CALIFORNIA AND THE WEST

Charis Wilson and Edward Weston

CALIFORNIA AND THE WEST

with 64 photographs by Edward Weston

foreword to the new, revised edition by Charis Wilson

An Aperture Book 1978

California and the West is published in a limited edition of three hundred fifty copies,
signed by Charis Wilson. This limited edition is accompanied by a silver print, Juniper / Tenaya Lake, 1937,
made from the original negative under the supervision of Cole Weston.

For those persons interested in reading other books on Edward Weston, Aperture has published
Edward Weston: Fifty Years, the definitive volume of his photographic work;
Daybooks of Edward Weston: Volume I, Mexico and Volume II, California;
Edward Weston: The Flame of Recognition, edited by Nancy Newhall; and Edward Weston: Nudes.

The prints for reproduction were provided by Cole Weston, Edward Weston's son
and executor, whose devotion to his father's work made possible the production of this book.

Aperture, Inc., publishes a periodical, portfolios, and books to communicate with serious
photographers and creative people everywhere.
A complete catalogue and information about subscriptions to the periodical will be mailed upon request.
Address: Millerton, New York 12546

Design by Jane Byers Bierhorst
The text of California and the West has been reproduced in its entirety from the original edition.
Printed by Halliday Lithographic Corporation, West Hanover, Massachusetts.
Bound by Sendor Bindery, New York City / Manufactured in the United States of America.
Cover: "Chief," Heggens' Barn / Salinas

To The John Simon Guggenheim Memorial Foundation

and Henry Allen Moe

Contents

Photographs

Foreword

A few years ago, on the way to an Edward Weston Retrospective at The Museum of Modern Art in New York, I rose from the subway depths, looked across the street, and saw a cluster of posters that brought me to a stop. Pasted to the soiled city wall was a picture of a young girl, swathed head to foot in protective camping garb. Her knees were akimbo, hands crossed loosely between her legs, and she looked straight at the viewer. She was a study in composure, but mine was momentarily shaken. I was looking at myself, as I had sat for a moment forty years earlier, and more than 3,000 miles away.

That picture provokes some gratifying—and some curious—reactions. One friend who obtained a copy remarked, "You don't do anything and come across twice as sexy." Then there was the critic who determined that the sexuality was symbolized by the indentations in the rock wall behind me. For a time, people would approach and say, "I recognized you at once from the picture in your book." Nowadays, along with other vintage Westons of me, it is taken to be a picture of my daughter.

On that long ago day the photographer, his friend Ansel Adams, and I, had been battling mosquitos and clambering about on a High Sierra mountain. The high country was backyard-familiar to Ansel, but Edward was having his first encounter with this crisp clean world of snow-polished roots and boulders, 13,000-foot cliffs patched with snow, and a mountain lake with floating islands of ice—even in July! Before the day was over he had made 24 negatives—the full load he carried for his 8 x 10 view camera—and one of them was the picture of me in my insect-proof headgear. The serenity he captured was in fact exhaustion, induced by too much activity at too high an altitude. But I know, and the picture reminds me, that in spite of mosquitos I was thoroughly enjoying myself.

When I go to have my eyes checked these days, the optometrist holds up a rod at a distance and moves it slowly toward my nose, saying: "Tell me when you see two." What happens then is much like the trick by which age splits us apart from our youthful self image. One day we recall some of our early activities with guilty embarrassment; the next day the split occurs and we can look with tolerance and even affection at 'that young creature' for whom we no longer bear the burden of responsibility.

This pleasant emancipation, which now permits me to look at the photograph, Charis at Lake Ediza, with amused approval, also makes me more appreciative of the book that emerged from Edward's and my travels in California and neighboring states in 1937 and 1938. These expeditions were courtesy of the Guggenheim Foundation, which had just awarded its first grant for photography to Edward. My tasks were to index every negative, to keep track of every penny spent, and to put down everything that happened in a log.

That log grew to about 700 pages and provided the raw material for California and the West. Whenever Edward was set up for a while along the road, I whipped out my light-weight Royal Signet, placed it on the front fender of our Ford, and went on with my detailed record. The resulting log—like its author—tends to be opinionated and dogmatic, crude on occasion, devoted to making fun of middle-class foibles, and enamored of pictorial detail. But it reflects with remarkable faithfulness Edward's views and likes and dislikes. Also, as I read back through the book I wrote, I find it full of the flavor of our journeying days.

Like anything written in the heat—and, in this instance, the rain, cold and windstorm—of the moment, there were things left unsaid. Some omissions were matters of taste. But there were other details and impressions of that fruitful period in Edward's life that could only have come into perspective with the passage of time.

One of the things left unsaid was that after the second trip my participation in the project became rather doubtful. One trip with Cole Weston and a second with his brother, Brett, had convinced me that I was not equipped for a year of that kind of travel. There was no private life with Edward, nor did I like being tucked in the back seat with the baggage because "the boys" preferred to do most of the driving. Edward did not drive.

When my twenty-third birthday fell in the interval between trips two and three, Edward still seemed ready to have young Westons along whenever they were available. I wrote him an impassioned pillow note on the subject, making my feelings clear. Finding this note preserved among Edward's papers, his biographer, Ben Maddow, interpreted it as a demand for marriage. But Edward knew that all I wanted was to cut him loose from his giant fledglings so that we could be full partners in the enterprise before us. In my youthful egocentricity, I did not doubt that what was best for me was likewise best for him. I knew I was a powerful persuader.

I still wince at the title of the book. Who but an Eastern publisher could imagine that one side trip into Oregon and Washington and another into Arizona and New Mexico, combined with a brief sortie across the Nevada border, added up to The

10

West? As I recall, it was a working title, but no improvement came to mind in time, and so there it stands, awkward and inaccurate.

My chagrin is partly compensated by the unembellished opening, simply the letter from the Guggenheim Foundation. The publishers pleaded for an introductory sentence, to make it smoother. But I resisted as adamantly as I knew how. "The letter," I wrote to them, "was the beginning, so that's where it begins."

Actually, that $2,000 grant spelled salvation. During the past two bottom depression years we had been scrimping along in Santa Monica Canyon. There were few sittings, and print sales—at $15 each, $10 to friends!—were widely spaced. Edward felt, with real desperation, that he might no longer be able to make a living from his own work. For months he had had to spend excruciating hours copying amateurish WPA paintings, just to keep the household in beans.

The Guggenheim permitted a year of frugal living and of liberated photographing. The funds were amplified by the Westways contract, paying $50 to Edward for eight to ten pictures a month and another $15 to me for commentary and captions. It was the magazine arrangement that enabled us to buy a new car.

From the vantage point of several decades, the amounts of money that one once sweated over seem small, even quaint. I cannot resist giving the car figures because they look so improbable. We paid $400 down on a brand new, 85 horsepower, Ford V-8 touring sedan. Financed at four and a half per cent by the Auto Club, our $42.01 monthly payments on Heimy—nicknamed in honor of the Guggenheim—were completed in a year. Total cost, $904.12!

Our expense records on the road also give some insight into the needs and tastes of the people who journeyed about in that Ford, as well as the domestic economics of the times. In April 1937, just before leaving on the second desert trip, we spent a total of $33.97 on supplies and food for three people. This included major outlays of $10.82 for a tarpaulin and $4.07 for the sturdy boots that I'm wearing in the poster photograph. Fruits and vegetables, mostly canned and dried, made up the bulk of the grocery supplies. The day-by-day reckoning en route was as follows:

Date	Location		
April 26	Glendale	9.5 gals gas	$ 1.67
		1 lb Sontag tobacco	.43
		1 pack pipe cleaners	.04
	29 Palms	8 gals gas	1.56
April 28	Amboy	cottage cheese, honey, cigarettes, matches	.75
		5.4 gals gas	1.50

April 29	29 Palms	avocados/buttermilk	.37
		Modess	.25
		7.2 gals gas	1.41
April 30	Mecca	4.5 gals gas	.88
		food and fork	1.23
		dates	.25
May 1	Calipatria	buttermilk, milk, apples	.84
		5.5 gals gas	1.08
May 2	Des. T. Post	4.5 gals gas	.88
		date milk shakes	1.30
		dates, fruit, datecakes	1.10
		showers	.50
		Camels	.30
May 3	Des. T. Post	milk shakes	.30
		cigarettes	.30
	Hemet	food	.51
		dates, avocados	.70
		13.5 gals gas	2.34

$20.49 (of which $11.32 is for gas)

As I totted up the figures later, that eight-day trip covered 850 miles; Heimy averaged 17.5 miles per gallon; and the daily cost of food per person, including cigarettes, was $.72. The trip also resulted in 59 negatives.

The tobacco was for our pipes. Mine was a lovely curved-stem affair, a gift from our British friend, John Davenport. I awoke one morning and was horrified to find it missing. I scoured the campsite before we left. Later, while Edward and Brett took photographs, I systematically unpacked and searched the car. It wasn't there. I drove back to the campsite, which was not easy to find in country where all sandy little side roads look alike, and sifted through the campfire ashes and crawled between boulders. I finally found the pipe nestled under a rock that leaned on a smaller one. It was a long time before I realized it must have found its way into that niche in the jaws of a pack rat.

One item on the pre-trip shopping list that evokes strong, pleasant memories is: "4 lbs coffee . . . $.88." Edward always bought unground coffee and had it pulverized. One of his prized possessions was his coffee pot. It was a dual container device. The coffee was placed in the (upside down) top chamber, and rapidly boiling water was poured quickly onto it. After one fast stir, the opening was covered with a piece of muslin, the bottom of the pot inverted over it and pressed down, and the edge of the muslin, protruding all around, helped seal the joint. The pot was then turned right-side up, and the screw in the middle of the top untwisted. Through a hole in the side of the screw, and down its hollow stem, the air rushed into the top and whooshed the coffee into the bottom. Once we gave our aluminum model a good scrubbing and discovered from the stamped identification on the bottom that the pot was called a Kin-Hee, and was made by the Hekin Company somewhere in Ohio. It was Edward's theory that this simplest and best of all coffee-makers had been rejected by the American housewife on account of the reusable cloth filter which gradually turned from dull tan to dark brown—too unhygienic. The only people I ever knew who had Kin-Hee pots were old friends of Edward's.

Food becomes a passionate interest when you are moving around. As described in the book, we started off each day with a quick bracing cup of coffee. Breakfast usually came at midmorning, after a couple of hours of work or driving, and lunch set in whenever hunger called for it. We equipped ourselves with dried fruit and nuts to tide us over between meals. Edward considered it a sin to waste good daylight by cooking, so we usually took our ready-to-eats in hand or aluminum cup—dry cereal, canned or fresh fruit, crackers, cheese, nutbutters, sardines. The secondary function of these meals was to break up the long days and bring us together for some rest and talk. After the light was gone came the hot meal, a quickly prepared but delicious mixture of canned goods. A typical stew recipe called for: a jar of chicken egg noodles, cans of corn, tomatoes and tamales, with some jack cheese melted on top. Any surplus was stored in the jar and added to the next night's stew. Our friend, Merle Armitage, later published a fancy cookbook entitled Fit for a King, and included five of our camp recipes as an appendix. Describing the corned-beef hash used in one dish, he wrote: it "comes out of the can like dog food."

The simple fare was relieved by local specialties along the way, such as date milk shakes, fresh lake trout, or the nearly black locust honey we discovered one day in a grocery in Julian. Then, too, there was the odd bit of luck, such as the memorable feast we had just after New Year's 1939 at the fashionable Furnace Creek Inn in Death Valley. The proprietress, a capable-looking gray-haired lady named Miss Ronan, had asked Edward to show prints to her guests. Despite our rough desert attire—the only clothing we had—she insisted that we return the following night as dinner guests. From the lordly bill of fare, we selected delicacies such as cream of artichoke soup, broiled lamb chops, sirloin of beef, creamed spinach, and fell upon the meal with appetites enlarged by two weeks of camp life. There was no check, but we paid for it after all.

At the meal's end, Miss Ronan informed us that we would be entertained by a gentleman who was delivering a lecture and showing a film about the Redwood

Empire. The screen was so wrinkled and the film so poor that the redwoods appeared as one long blur. This did not dim the speaker's enthusiasm, though. He told us about the businessman who walked among the trees and lost all his worries, and also about the virtues of building with cutdown redwood trees as lumber. He adjured us to walk among the trees, to talk to them, and to let them talk to us. Then, without warning, he burst into song,—an off-key tremolo rendering of the tune set to Joyce Kilmer's poem, "Trees." We sat in stunned silence until he wavered to the penultimate dramatic line, "Poems are made by fools like me . . ." then dashed to the doorway before the lights came on, with a hasty thanks to Miss Ronan for our meal, and out into the night and beyond.

Our standard of living on the road also took great leaps forward when we visited Ansel Adams or when he came to see us, invariably bearing steaks and liquor. Edward and Ansel had been good friends since the late Twenties, and the similarities and differences between the two men were interesting to observe. Ansel was clean-shaven then and towered above Edward. Both men were lean, sinewy and extremely agile as they set about their work.

Edward usually felt that we became too leisurely when we had company: it made him jumpy. Ansel was much the same way. He and Edward incited each other, and they would take after photographic quarry like two differently trained hounds, each following the scent that was right for him. They seemed to enjoy a trace of competition between them and egging each other on, but they were very compatible.

It was a particularly interesting period in their relationship because Edward was, so to speak, invading Ansel's turf—Yosemite and the High Sierra. When we were at Lake Ediza, there was an interesting campfire discussion about the effect of height on the individual photographer's viewpoint. The log records:

> Edward says after he did his last negative last night, Ansel set up and focussed as he would have done it. Edward liked Ansel's way better but never could have seen it that way himself, not being tall enough.

Visits to Ansel's and Virginia's home in Yosemite often led to hilarious evenings. Ansel was a wonderful raconteur, pianist and mime. I vividly remember him standing straight up, one arm at his side and the other pointing ahead, turning in a tight circle with his eyes shut, and opening one eye each time he rotated toward you. A lighthouse. Another memorable Adams performance was his piano rendition of <u>Love for Three Oranges,</u> in which he chased three real oranges up and down the keyboard as he played. Edward was a quieter man. He enjoyed telling stories but they were likely to be set pieces and I had soon heard them all. Possibly Virginia felt the same way about Ansel's, but his were new to me.

In the aftermath of Ansel's darkroom fire, when we were working as a salvage crew on the negatives, Edward had been amazed at the number of fine images that Ansel had never found time to print. Now it looked as though he would soon be in the same boat. When were these hundreds of negatives, piling up in a storage warehouse, to be given their viewing form?

Edward maintained there was no sense wasting the chance to make more negatives by cutting short our travels, and I was inclined to agree. It had taken several trips to work the bugs out of our camping procedures and eliminate most of the photographic hazards. By mid-year we could take to the road with confidence that we were prepared for whatever might befall, but where was the sense in having developed all this savvy if we were to make no further use of it? On the other hand, the more negatives made, the more printing to be done! The best solution we could come up with was to apply for a year's renewal of the fellowship, planning to split it 50/50 between printing and more travel. Most of the photographers we talked it over with—Willard Van Dyke, Imogen Cunningham, Ansel Adams, among them—thought it was a splendid idea. A few, including a famous documentary photographer, disagreed, and to this day I cannot understand why. Perhaps they thought it would be in bad taste to ask for so much. There is also the possibility that the Guggenheim award put a formal stamp of legitimacy on photography as an art form, and that this made some of its practitioners uneasy. In any event, the Guggenheim Committee of Selection agreed to the extension.

I like to think the Committee was dazzled by my intensive record-keeping that provided them with detailed lists of negatives made, supplies purchased, miles traveled, as well as over-all exposition of Western territory. Our early trips through bare-bones desert country had made me a geography enthusiast. I, who had once seen a range of hills on the horizon as a more or less interesting set of curves, now wanted to find out how they had been formed, what effect they had on local weather, etc. A legacy from those days still has me searching—whenever I drive toward mountains— for that all-important pass that determines the route of water, people and vehicles.

Our friend Zohmah, later Dorothy Charlot, was the only passenger we took on a trip who provided me with a ready-made log. I have quoted excerpts in the book, but here is her general view of us at the time:

> Edward and Charis know how to live. Among other things, they can make the least effort of routines and do completely the things they like. Good dinner was ready in a moment and then slow, leisurely eating and sipping of hot Weston special deluxe coffee and fun conversation about, briefly, "Ye Gods, how can a writer write? How when he comes up against a place like the desert can he speak of it with words found alphabetically arranged in every dictionary?"

Edward said when he used to write there were not enough words for beauty. Charis said maybe it is best not to try and tell about things; we can really say only what things do to us. . . Charis, though, besides being a sophisticate, a bohemian, is also a 'child of nature' and could walk about casually in the blackened world.

Edward, of course, can only be touched by beauty. Like his camera-eye, he is separated from all blight and time and ordinary dimensions. So he isn't brave like Charis, just superior.

I was secretly bewitched by Zohmah's description of me: it was how I saw myself.

The event that wound up the second year goes unmentioned in the book. On April 24th, 1939, arriving in the coast town of Elk, we looked up an official named Judge Walker. He turned out to be a delightful old man with a peg leg and a white beard, as well as a former portrait photographer. The conversation was recorded in the log:

Edward / Can you do some marrying for us?
Judge W. / Well, I'm not dressed for it. Got these dirty old cords on because I was shucking abalones. . .
Edward / Oh, that's all right. We've been camping, so we just have our boots and pants on. . .
Judge W. / (In his living room, with his wife as witness and his book open in hand) How much of this do you want me to read?
Edward / Just whatever you want to, Judge. We'll leave it up to you.

And so, with our pair of well-worn gold rings from a pawnshop, the papers completed, and Judge Walker in possession of $2.50, Edward and I were married.

Friends often reacted with amazement and horror to the details of our simplified camp-life. The very thought of sleeping on the ground without an air mattress, having no table to prepare food and eat on, and managing at night without a Coleman lantern, brought on a case of shudders, and a "How do you stand it?" I used to smile wisely, and say, "You get used to it," which no one could have considered an informative response. The explanation lay in what made mere comfort secondary: Edward's work.

Memory is a great simplifier. I am astonished, reading back through the moment by moment account in the log, at the steady stream of mishaps and problems that had to be overcome in order to create those clear, untroubled—occasionally comic—images that Edward achieved. At location after location, the light was wrong, the wind was too strong, it was raining. Winter-blanketed trees would dump heaps of snow onto Edward and his camera at exactly the wrong moment. The waves would break perfectly over coastal rocks—and his camera shutter would refuse to function. We visited and revisited what became—in our minds—the jinxed chicken coops between Valley Ford and Tomales in Marin County. These irregular gray constructions, with their broken necklace of white birds scattered on the bare hillside, drew Edward like a magnet, but the light was always wrong. If it wasn't too foggy or too late and dark, it was too hot and sunny and the chickens stayed inside. Once the light was right and the chickens were out, but a lethargic group of cows kept ambling in and out of the scene.

We would return to such sites, that tantalized but never quite fulfilled their promise, only if we were already heading in that direction. Otherwise Edward was too impatient to see new territory to keep revisiting familiar scenes. Nor would he wait very long anywhere for a change of light. He'd say: "I might be missing something better five miles up the road, and the light may be perfect for it right now!" More often than not it happened that way. We climbed a hill, or rounded a turn, and there it would be. You could feel the electricity in the car—the kind of excitement sometimes generated in a gambling casino—and the moment I pulled off the road Edward would be hauling out the tripod, lengthening its legs, and screwing the 8 x 10 onto it. While his hands performed these mechanical tasks, his eyes kept returning to the critical area: which lens element was needed? What about a filter? Where would he put the camera? All these decisions were made—and often a negative as well—in a couple of minutes. The equipment was big and clumsy, but Edward could work with astonishing speed.

Then came the moment of rest, with Edward always asking—quite unnecessarily—"Do you want to see?" I was so used to looking on the ground glass that I saw the image right-side up, and was as foolishly surprised as Edward to be reminded it wasn't when someone else said, "Why, it's upside down!" I even made some progress toward seeing black and white equivalents instead of the lovely opalescent colors the ground glass showed. "Weston country" I could spot with no difficulty, and often I could narrow down to the general area of a negative; but to see 'the real thing' on the ground glass always produced a special kind of surprise. It was as if someone had turned the scene of a picnic into a memorable sonnet right before your eyes.

My dominant memory of that two-year adventure is of the confident anticipation with which we traveled, and the ever-present excitement of the chase. Edward had always known he had an inexhaustible camera eye. If we hit a dull stretch, it couldn't last long. Over the next rise of ground, off the next dirt track, or through the door of an abandoned shack just up the way, the next picture was waiting for him to come and find it.

Charis Wilson
Aptos, California
September, 1978

1 Death Valley

Initiation

JOHN SIMON GUGGENHEIM MEMORIAL FOUNDATION

551 FIFTH AVENUE ● NEW YORK

March 18, 1937

Dear Mr. Weston:

I am delighted to write you that today the Trustees, on the nomination of the Committee of Selection, appointed you to a Fellowship of the Foundation in the following terms:

Project: The Making of a Series of Photographs of the West

Period: Twelve months from April 1st, 1937

Stipend: Two Thousand Dollars . . . .

AFTER five months of cross-fingered suspense, there it was. Now we could drop the capital If that had prefaced our plotting and planning all winter. We pinched ourselves and each other, executed calisthenics appropriate to the occasion, and set about translating the plans into fact.

For the next three weeks we lived in bedlam. The two-room house that was to be our Los Angeles base was already stacked to the roof with our furniture and sundry possessions. Now, as newly bought items of equipment were brought home, the living space in the center of the rooms diminished to a narrow lane between bed, bath, and kitchen sink. We were doubly grateful to friends who, nearly every night, asked us out to farewell dinners; eating at home would have meant stand-up supper.

Concerning what to take, where to go, and what to go in, we received abundant advice. Our friends argued the advantages of station wagon over trailer, or vice versa; told us about their pet Kollapsible Kamp Kots, and where there were restaurants off the beaten track that served good chicken dinners. One man wrote to Edward saying he was naming one of his new race horses after him and if Edward wanted to risk a little on a 40-to-1 shot that was a sure thing. . . .

Most of our advisors failed to consider one important factor: the limited elasticity of two thousand dollars. As the most casual amateur swiftly learns, photography is expensive. Edward's equipment is simplicity itself, but take the single item of films: 8x10's—by the case—come to twenty-seven cents apiece. In the months we had spent planning this campaign (*If*), we had distributed and redistributed the dollars and cents until they made for a maximum of photography and travel. Trailers and station wagons had been dropped early in the reckoning, and along with them hotels, autocamps, and restaurants.

By following the seasons we expected to camp out most of the time. We got cheap kapok sleeping bags and a small tent, the latter for use when it rained or when we wanted to maintain a permanent camp for a while. But the back-to-nature movement was to stop short of camp cooking; to save all the daylight hours for photography we needed food that could be simply and quickly prepared. Canned food was to be our mainstay, supplemented with ready-to-eats such as dried fruits, cheese, crackers, honey, nut butter. A two-burner gasoline stove, a nest of cooking pots and plates, and a thermos made up the culinary equipment; a bucket, a five-gallon desert waterbag, a pint canteen, shovel and axe, railroad lantern and flashlight, completed our outfit. Total cost: $50.00.*

When we said we were going to get a reliable secondhand car, our friends hooted the adjective and told us fearful tales of crankcases full of sawdust and engines held together with rubber bands and chewing gum. We examined a few of the consumptive jalopies that fitted inside our budget figure and began to despair. Then fortune smiled again. Phil Hanna, editor of the Southern California Auto Club magazine, *Westways*, had been mapping out some routes for us with road and weather notes. When we went to get them, he said he wanted to have eight or ten pictures a month in the magazine as we went along. Our problem was solved. Within an hour we were picking out a new Ford V-8 sedan, and incidentally, in the excitement, making our first mistake by saving a few dollars on a black paint job. There were many scorching desert days in which we regretted that saving.

This sleek new beauty, which we promptly christened Heimy, was to lead a strenuous life. Aside from brief stays under civilized roofs when we would put in to Los Angeles or San Francisco for developing and reprovisioning, Heimy would be our only home for a long time to come. Edward had originally planned to print at

---

*This included three sleeping bags. Later additions—a tarpaulin, two two-gallon canteens, metal tent-stakes—brought the total to $65.00.

least some of his negatives as he went along. But now that we had a dependable car which could be trusted on the worst backroads of the hinterland, it would be foolish not to concentrate on seeing as much of California as we could in a year. Except for *Westways'* ten pictures a month, printing could wait.

Hanna had mapped six skeleton trips which we expected to embroider on as fancy led or weather dictated. To begin with, Death Valley. The season there ends May first due to the unconscionable heat, so we set ourselves a deadline and worked against it. On the eve of our departure we settled down to the serious business of hair-cutting. Edward had barbered his sons for years, and vice versa, but my shoulder-length tresses filled him with alarm and uncertainty. Although I insisted I wanted it so short that none could get in my eyes, he would cautiously remove only an inch at a time, at each stage demanding to know if that wasn't really short enough. When the hazardous operation had at last been brought to a successful conclusion we spread out the maps to examine our route, reading off the wonderful names: Calico Mountains, Bicycle Lake, Owl's Head Mountains, Dripping Spring, Old Confidence Mill—every square inch of the desert was filled with compelling nomenclature.

Cole, Edward's youngest son*, was going with us, and next morning the three of us worked from six until nine-thirty getting the car packed with a non-listing load and sufficient passenger room. Then we started off through the endless Los Angeles suburbs and out Foothill Boulevard.

In less than an hour came the first halt, Edward out to examine rows of short black grape stumps laid out on yellow sand; but there was too much haze to suit him. There must be more and better vineyards to come. We moved on. Actually, two years were to intervene before we found the right field of grape stumps. In a few minutes another halt, and this time it was up-camera for the first Guggenheim negative: a crab-apple tree, in a full coat of snowball blossoms, alone in the middle of a green field. Taking my job as recorder seriously, I wrote down that this history-making event happened forty-six miles from Glendale on U. S. No. 66. On subsequent trips over that road we watched for the tree but we never saw it again; evidently it had fulfilled its destiny and departed hence.

The San Gabriel Mountains and the San Bernardinos were sparkling with snow as we climbed up between them over Cajon Pass and rolled down onto the Mojave Desert. To be sure of a good camping place on our first night out, as well as for old times' sake, we decided to make for Deadmans Point where Edward had worked a

---

*To keep the record straight, there are four in all: Chandler, Brett, Neil, Cole, in descending scale from 27 to 18. We used Chandler's house and darkroom for our Los Angeles base, Brett's in San Francisco.

few years before. This one (for the California deserts are strewn with Deadmens Points) is an acre or so of piled-up granite boulders rising from the flat Mojave a dozen miles from Victorville. We reached it in mid-afternoon and drove Heimy into a secluded place between the towering rocks.

Cole set out with his gun to look for big game or tin cans; Edward set up his camera and went to work on the scenery. Although I had never been there before, the surroundings were familiar, since I could recognize Westons on every hand: a sloping finger of rock at the base of the main stack; a group of round boulders, one balanced alarmingly, near the top of the pile; and, across the road, a flat-topped rocky cliff with a curving sandy track leading back to it. I had never seen that last print without wanting to walk up the twisty road, and now at last I could.

Cole made the photographic find of the day: on the edge of a dry lake across the road, a beautiful dead buzzard. The sun was near setting and a breeze had come up, so Edward had difficulty with the ruffling feathers, but he finally got what he wanted. Then we all climbed into Heimy and went skimming madly over the glass-like surface of the dry lake, startling a couple of wide-eyed cows that were straying around the far end of it.

At sundown the breeze increased to a cold steady wind. We gathered sticks, built a fire in the shelter of the rocks, and by its heartening glow consumed our first camp supper. Edward climbed into Heimy to un- and reload his film-holders, while Cole and I draped the windows with blankets and sleeping bags weighted down with provisions. Just as everything was well secured the wind, which had relented for a while, gave a sudden blast—the draperies flew off and boots and canned goods went clattering down a gully in the dark. For the duration of the darkroom period, Cole and I were obliged to stand on the running boards holding down the covers with numbing fingers.

We built up the fire and warmed ourselves, then unrolled the sleeping bags and spread them at the foot of the cliff. For a while the flashlight was passed back and forth as each of us in turn discovered some sharp hard object lodged under the middle of his back. Then we lay looking up at the thousands of sharp, glittering stars, picking out Ursa Major and Minor—as far as any of us could go in that direction—and exclaiming at shooting stars that were so many and brilliant it was hard to stop looking and go to sleep.

Five o'clock in the morning is a chill hour on the Mojave when no thinking person would get out of a warm sleeping bag, except he be beguiled by the aroma of hot coffee—especially Weston coffee, for Edward's technique with that sensitive beverage is equalled only by his way with a camera. Thanks to the cold, our car-packing time was cut down by a good three hours from the previous morning, and we moved off across the desert in a postcard sunrise until a flowering Joshua tree called for a stop.

While Edward was working, a man drove up in a wheezy rattletrap. First he asked if Edward were a "real photographer"; being assured that such was the case, he asked if Edward would photograph his wrecked car a few miles down the road. "You see the lawyer wants it to show the insurance people just how it happened. I could pay you for it . . . I've taken eight snapshots with my kodak but I'd rather have it done [pointing to the 8x10] with one of those machines." Edward said he'd be glad to do it but he didn't expect to get to printing any of his negatives for a year. The man said that was too bad because he could have paid for it and there weren't any photographers in Victorville so maybe he'd better make a few more snapshots, and with a last admiring look for the big camera he rattled away.

As we drove along, the Mojave spread out before us clear and clean under the bright morning sky. Over its undulating surface an army of greasewood marched in neat formation, each scraggly green bush jealously guarding its little circle of soil. Above these even ranks an occasional Joshua tree stuck out its bristling elbows, or groups of Joshuas stood together gesticulating wildly. In the distance there were always piles of bare wrinkled mountains, rising so abruptly from the desert floor and cutting such clean sharp profiles in the sky they looked like painted backdrops.

When we turned north at Baker, we left the pavement and the open country behind. Dark rocky peaks shut off the distance and the greasewood areas were broken up by ridges of tan-colored mud-hills. Cole had the wheel and I glanced out the back window to make an astonishing discovery. A large blue lake, on whose shining surface the surrounding mountaintops were clearly reflected, had replaced most of the landscape we had just driven through. So we encountered our first mirage and began to feel exceedingly desert-wise.

About noon of the third day we passed Death Valley Junction and started the last lap into the valley from the east side. The road climbed over an easy pass and coasted down to the checking station that marks the National Monument's boundary. Down Furnace Creek Wash the main road continued, between cliffs of orange, yellow, and brown, to the floor of the valley. But right beside the checking station was the road leading up to Dantes View, and we had to satisfy our curiosity about that view. Two of our friends who had been there had told Edward he probably wouldn't like it because everything was so far away. The picture reproduced in the official Death Valley folder was by no means inspiring, but it suggested possibilities. Heimy was forced to climb the roughest mile in creation; his back tires frequently lost their footing and when we reached the turnaround on top he was running a temperature of 212°. However, the reward was out of all proportion to the difficulties of ascent.

North and south the valley seemed to extend to infinity—harsh barefaced mountains hemming in the narrow trough. More than a mile below us, spread over half the valley's width, lay a glistening salt bed, with tapering ribbons of white extending from its sides. The dazzling white lake was bordered with a fringe of feathery grey that melted into a background of deep chocolate brown. At the base of the cliff we stood on, the neat arc of an alluvial fan was rimmed by a fine black line which we presently realized must be a highway. Across the valley rose the seamed scarred wall of the Panamints, with sweeping curves of vast alluvial aprons at its base and a sparkling coat of snow on its peaks.

A hundred miles of desolate geography spread out below us in the weighty silence peculiar to deserts. We might have been on a lost moon world where time and motion had ceased to exist. Edward was so shaky with excitement he could hardly set up his camera, and all that any of us could say for some time was "My God! It can't be!" But other cars drove up and their occupants were vocal enough. When I had looked my fill, I listened.

Three women and a man got out of a car, walked to the railing, and looked over.

FIRST WOMAN: "Well! I never expected it to look like this!"

SECOND WOMAN: "You know, that name 'Death Valley' sort of kills the place. Who'd want to go to a place with a name like that?"

THIRD WOMAN (turning back toward car): "Is this as high as Yellowstone was?" They all walked back to the car arguing about just how high Yellowstone was.

That night we camped among the mud-hills up an ABANDONED—TRAVEL AT YOUR OWN RISK road. We had driven down 20-Mule Team Canyon, the road a curving dry wash between pale ochre hills, the hills pitted with tunnel openings where borax had been taken out. But our own campsite was enough to wonder at, with a cliff rising above it impossible to believe: rose-red at the top, melting into orange, and orange into pale green (somehow managed with no offense but rather delight to the eye), then down to a dozen varied shades of brown and yellow. If we looked in the other direction, there were smooth-shaped yellow mud-cliffs straggling across the wide grey gravel of Furnace Creek Wash; beyond that, dark massed peaks of the Funeral Range.

The next day began well with Zabriskie Point, which proved the perfect complement to Dantes View. The turnaround was built on the crest of a low mud-hill and the effect was something like standing on the stage of an outdoor theater and looking up at the tiers of seats. But here you looked up at, and out over, ridge on ridge of bright-colored mud-hills, red, yellow, brown, and a hundred intermediate shades all of which changed with the light from hour to hour.

Zabriskie Point is a great favorite with snapshooters who dash up, snap, and dash away, faster than you can keep count. A man and wife drove up, climbed out of their car, and stared at the view. The man scrutinized Edward's outfit and approached with, "If I took a picture of that stuff with my kodak, it would be flat, wouldn't it?"

"Not much contrast there now," Edward allowed.

The woman speaks: "Come on, let's go. I've had enough of Death Valley. [*Adding hastily*] Of course, it's beautiful . . . and interesting . . . but it's . . . but it's . . ." While she struggles for the word that will not come, the man asks if they can see Mt. Whitney from here. We say they'd have to go up to Dantes View on a clear day to see it. As they start back to their car, the woman's groping is rewarded. "*It's weird!*" she calls back to us triumphantly. Edward is dug halfway into the back of the car looking for his lens shade and I am standing on the stone rampart gazing out over the mud-hills. But the woman is too happy with her word to care. "Weird," she murmurs again. "That's what it is. It's just plain weird."

This day marked a change in our desert fortunes. Perhaps things had gone too well thus far and the desert resented our easy assumption of familiarity. At any rate, wrong things began to happen in rapid succession. It started with the weather, close and muggy, when by all Death Valley rules it should have been hot and dry. Then we tore a hole in our desert waterbag, which meant we must lodge in the public campground until we replaced it. And there were our dwindling food supplies. We had planned to restock as needed en route, but a brief inspection of prices at the Furnace Creek store made it clear that any buying there would seriously unbalance the budget.

The little settlement at Furnace Creek is under the aegis of the Pacific Coast Borax Company. There is a de luxe inn with swimming pool and golf course, a store and tourist cabins, an airplane landing, a date grove, and a couple of gas stations. At first we were inclined to make considerable fun of this bit of transplanted Palm Springs set down among the clean bare cliffs. We were more than dismayed at the prices: twenty-seven cents for a gallon of gas and fifteen cents for a tiny head of lettuce. But there was a compensation. At the end of a day of sticky, oppressive heat we dove into the pool—clear blue water, soft as jelly, and gently warm as it comes from the springs. At that moment we could have overlooked a putting green in every dry wash.

Hanna had given us a letter to Don Curry, the Park naturalist (really a geologist). Through him we had some food and a canteen brought in from the Junction. He apologized for the muggy weather which he assured us was most unusual and couldn't last. He drove us around and pointed out lots of geology—almost everything seemed to be volcanic tuff. He suggested some fine places for Edward to work, except that all the roads happened to be washed out.

But of all the places he thought Edward should see, Curry was most enthusiastic about Butte Valley up in the Panamints. There, he told us, was a large butte with black and white stripes zigzagging across its face. After Dantes View and Zabriskie Point, we could believe anything. The last part of the road being too rough for Heimy we would have to complete the trip in Curry's vehicle, an International pick-up, but a black-and-white-striped butte sounded worth a little discomfort.

The first part of the trip, across the valley and south to Bennetts Well, was accomplished without incident. There we left Heimy picketed among the mesquites. Edward and I wedged into the front seat of the pick-up, while Cole braced himself in the open back among camera cases, canteens, and food, with a sleeping bag for a shock absorber. Off down the road we rattled and banged until—a plunge, a lurch, a sagging stop—and there went a rear wheel bouncing away among the greasewood. Someone—Curry named him in terms far from endearing—had merely tossed the wheel on, completing the good job by leaving the tools out. It was a cheering discovery to make in mid-desert, with Bennetts Well ten miles away by then and nothing around us but greasewood, horseflies, and heat.

"DESERT CLAIMS FOUR," I saw the splendid headline and read on, "A grim tragedy of the desert was unfolded here today as . . . ." Curry was calm about it (and so he should have been, since his nightly lecture at Furnace Creek always mentioned the fact that there was plenty of water in Death Valley if you knew where to look), but I noticed his first impulse, like ours, was to reach for the comfort of a full canteen.

We retrieved the wheel and a little searching turned up some of that omnipresent California commodity, baling wire. That served for pliers; a pick, hammer, and crowbar stood in for the other missing tools. An hour and a half's hot labor—Cole and Curry did the laboring while Edward and I whisked horseflies off their shirtless backs—and the vagrant member was on to stay.

After such an evil omen a sensible savage would have turned back, warned;

we continued southward and presently turned west up into the hills. Curry had exaggerated when he said the road was bad. There was no road. The pick-up ascended from boulder to boulder in a narrow, steeply winding creek bed, with such ear-splitting crashes and spine-shattering jolts I thought each moment would be our last as well as the pick-up's. Higher and higher we climbed. Wild flowers appeared, white, yellow, purple: Indian paintbrush, paper-bag plant, riotous apricot mallow. Bump, clatter, crash. On and up. Two wild burros, one a pinto, regarded our tuneful progress from a discreet distance. Curry told us of dining with a prospector in this region who had served him burro meat under the pseudonym of lamb stew.

Half a lifetime of jolting and banging and we came suddenly onto a comparatively smooth roadbed. The hills opened out and we could see, a mile or so away, a long bunker-shaped mass of dark rock. It had stripes along its side, to be sure—black and white stripes possibly—but of such a subdued nature as to attract little attention. This was the wonder-butte we had, almost literally, broken our necks to see. Undoubtedly, it was fine specimen geologically; photographically it was just a butte.

The next day we gave up. A close dirty sky shut down over the valley, locking in the humidity. Edward began to worry about his films, thinking they might not be adequately protected against such excesses of weather; our food supplies were again approaching vanishing point—so after a morning of halfhearted exploring we climbed up into the Panamints headed for home. We stopped once in the mountains while Edward bagged a monster zeppelin cloud that, steeped in sunset light, rested above the Panamints' summit. That was the picture of the day.

Next day we crossed the northern end of the Mojave with only a violent windstorm on Searles (dry) Lake to enliven the dullest stretch of the trip: mile after mile of rolling desert covered with the always evenly spaced greasewood bushes, not a hill or a tree or a house to break the bald monotony. Then we came to Red Rock Canyon.

I don't know if erosion is classed by the kind of formation it produces, but if it is this could only be called *cathedral type*: spires and buttresses, cloisters and choir-stalls, were cut into cliffs brick-red to rosy pink. We walked around looking and Edward said, "What can I do with it? It's all done. Photographing this stuff would be like copying a painting. Anyway, it's too damned pretty."

The afternoon was hazy, the sun hot. We were tired from long driving and our morning's bout with the wind. We found a sheltered-looking spot in a V of the cliffs, spread out our sleeping bags, and lay down for a nap. We were amused to find relics of a recent movie company, gaudy scraps of painted canvas stuck to the cliff sides. Evidently Red Rock Canyon hadn't looked too pretty to them, for they had retouched nature's efforts with a liberal hand.

It must have been the flapping of these canvas scraps that awakened us. We saw we were in for a blow and hurried to get supper underway before the elements should become unbearable, which they soon did. We loaded all blowables back into Heimy, rolled the windows up tight, and climbed in on top of the load clutching our plates of food. The miraculous gas stove had not blown out in the gale, but in the instant it took to transfer food from stew pan to plates the blowing sand had not been idle, and our dismal dinner was punctuated by the sound of crunching gravel.

In such a gale it would have been impossible to cover the car. Edward had to crouch on the floor with a blanket over him to load films. When the ordeal was over, he told us that no matter how slowly he pulled the slides, sparks had flown every time, so there was no knowing what would appear when the films were developed.

We surveyed the sleeping facilities with little enthusiasm. A shallow cave in a near-by cliff was the best that offered and Edward and I hauled our bags up to it. Cole came down with claustrophobia when he saw the low ceiling and decided that Heimy would give him shelter enough if he filled up the space below the running board with camera cases and boxes. All night the wind raged and howled among the cliffs, enriching the architectural detail by means of a heavy gravel spray. I burrowed to the lower depths of my sleeping bag to shut out the noise. Once in the night I came half awake to hear Edward mingling his profanities with those of the wind, and another time I thought people were throwing shoes at me but decided it must be a dream.

In the morning I was almost ashamed to admit I had slept. Edward had been kept awake all night by brickbats, he called them (those must have been the shoes), pelting down from the overhanging rocks. After spending half the night awake to hang onto his blanket, Cole had given up and spent the other half cramped in the car. In the cruel light of early dawn they were both tragic spectacles, but Weston coffee performed its magic and Edward was soon setting up his camera to meet the Red Rock challenge.

We followed up a long sub-canyon where the prevailing hue was a delicate olive-green and the erosion patterns were like rippled satin. There Edward worked all morning against a satanic wind that would die down to encourage him to make an exposure and blow up savagely the moment he had his slide out. I would hold grimly to a leg of the tripod to keep the camera from crashing over while Edward stood waiting and watching until at last an instant's calm would give him time to release the shutter.

That afternoon we returned to the Los Angeles base. In Mint Canyon the shock of the brilliant color of green grass hurt our eyes; but more severe, to the ear now adjusted to desert stillness, was the shock of city noise. We had not been prepared for it that time, but even on subsequent returnings, when we knew what to expect, we would always be re-amazed at the cacophony of blaring radios, squawking automobile horns, thundering trains, and shouting newsboys.

2 Mojave and Colorado Deserts
Granite and Sandstone

HAD it been in our power to choose the events that would break us in to our new scheme of life, we would doubtless have selected a gentler series. But that violent initiation had some distinct advantages. In a single week we had learned most of the hazards of desert travel; and, having seen in the first place the most magnificent possible desert scenery, we could now pass by many less exciting places that might otherwise have stopped us. Edward was forever afterward saying, "If I'd never seen Death Valley, I would probably work here."

The films had suffered no damage from heat but two were spoiled by fog streaks. It would have been a severe test of any camera's lightproofness—those ten-minute waits in the brilliant sun, the film unprotected in the camera, while Edward weighed his chances with the unco-operative wind. Now the 8x10 was decked out in a new red bellows, put on over the old one for double indemnity, and Edward invented a fancy system of punch-holes for the rebates of the film-holders so that if a negative were fogged in the future, the dots on the film rebate would indicate which side of which holder was guilty.

April twenty-sixth we set out again, this time taking Brett (who had come down from San Francisco) and starting down the southwestern edge of the Mojave. With a heavyweight tarpaulin to rope over the car at night for loading, an insulated wooden box to hold the films, two two-gallon canteens, and a full two-weeks' food supply, we were now prepared for all desert manifestations. As a concession to our advising public, which assured us we would quickly tire of canned food, we had taken a few potatoes to Death Valley. They returned to Los Angeles intact. It was too simple to blend the contents of several cans into a really magnificent stew; we couldn't be bothered with anything more complicated. We had also taken some magazines on the first trip but no one had any time to read them, so we dropped that refinement, too.

Our first objective this trip was the Joshua Tree National Monument that lies just east of the little San Bernardino Mountains. Heimy rolled east through the orange groves to San Bernardino, south down a green valley where cows stood contentedly knee-deep in ponds; through Redlands, Beaumont, and Banning; between the white-headed peaks of San Gorgonio and San Jacinto. Once he shied at a terrifying hundred-wheeled monster that threatened to crowd him from the pavement—a truck almost invisible under the cargo of bicycles it was bearing back to town from the Palm Springs season.

We left the highway and ran northeast across the desert to Twentynine Palms. That appeared to be a city of the future, consisting almost entirely of large signs advertising attractive homesites. The city fathers had evidently decided to begin with the outskirts and work in. The center of town was two gas stations—one active, one passive—and a drugstore. A mile or so north was the post office, half a mile south the grocery; between lay vast numbers of attractive homesites, if one had a weakness for uninterrupted vistas of greasewood. We found a touching evidence of civic pride a little distance from the "center." A diminutive plot of ground had been cleared, a simple, rustic pavilion erected, a half dozen stunted smoke trees set out. A modest sign proclaimed this SMOKE TREE PARK.

While approaching Twentynine Palms, we had seen a lavish display of desert granite off to the right but no roads leading to it. The man at the active gas station told us how to find the road and said that the place was called Rattlesnake Valley. It was really only half a valley: a long irregular cliff of tumbled granite with a scattering of separate piles in front of it, any one of which could have effaced Deadmans Point. And the setting here was less austere. Around the rock piles, the greasewood sea gave way to a foam of wild flowers and blooming cacti. Here we first saw *yucca mojavensis* —a junior edition of the Joshua tree with long white fibres curling off its dagger-leaves, so that the plant appears engaged in perpetual struggle with a spool of cotton thread. Jack rabbits bounded away at our approach; quail and mourning doves filled the air with gentle conversation; of the creature the place was named for there was no sign.

We camped there two nights. The first night we had a fine moonrise and a flurry of raindrops, both of which I slept through. In the sharp pre-sunrise cold we had our coffee by a blaze of greasewood trunks. Brett stood incautiously close and set the leg of his jeans on fire. A needle the size of a crowbar, a stout black thread, a folded blue bandanna for the patch—with these I performed an artistic repair job.

Brett and Edward wandered around photographing rocks; I just wandered. From the jagged crest above us, the granite blocks were tumbled down in wild disorder, and when I started climbing up the slope I found gaps where you could look down through the boulders to a dry river bed underneath. The mountainside of rocks was suspended over space and it looked as though one hearty shout would bring the whole thing down.

In the afternoon the wind came up and I retired to Heimy to bring the log up to date. Brett came along, set down his 8x10 on extended legs, and walked away for a moment. I saw a black fluttering pass the window and knew the worst. Surely no other inanimate thing can look as pitiful as a fallen camera—the tripod legs spread gawkily, the ground glass and lens board twisted out of line as if someone had wrung the poor creature's neck. Heimy's windows were rolled up tight, so if Brett indulged in colorful language I didn't hear it. After a while of tinkering, he decided a little glue would render it usable.

During dinner that night there was a scurrying behind the campfire which prompted us to leave our cheese rinds and lettuce scraps on the rock ledge. No sooner were we in our sleeping bags than a great commotion started up. We flashed the lantern on six fat mice who were devouring our offerings with hectic enthusiasm.

Next morning I had another job of pants-mending: the knees of Edward's leather riding breeches were suffering from a brief but poignant contact with a cholla cactus. The material was worn too fine for needle-and-thread work, and among our stores adhesive tape proved the only possible remedy. While I was thus engaged by the embers of the morning coffee fire, the first rays of sunlight struck the rocks above me. Instantly there was a noise of scrabbling claws and a scaly body. Prepared by a little desert reading between trips, I knew that the dark reptilian head poking out of the crevice belonged to a chuckwalla. And, according to the books, if I gave chase the big lizard would retire among the rocks and puff himself up so I couldn't dislodge him, but I didn't put that part to the test.

At the Twentynine Palms grocery we found glue for Brett's camera and met a pink kitten named Bobby. "Everyone's babied him," the proprietress told us fondly, "ever since he lost his tail in the frigidaire." The palm clump was visible from the store so Brett and I counted heads. I made it eighteen and a half, he made it twenty-two and a half. No one seemed to know what had happened to the other six or ten. After a cursory examination of our maps, I suggested that the Amboy crater wasn't far away and since there was a big lava flow around it perhaps we should go and look.

We followed a sandy track across a greasewood plain, up through a gap in the Sheep Hole Mountains, around a spur of the Bullions, across the Bristol Dry Lake. Luckily traffic was not heavy—each of the two cars we did meet left powdery dust sifting down on us for ten minutes after. We stopped once to let a desert tortoise cross

Evening Cloud / Panamints   33

36   Death Valley / from Dantes View

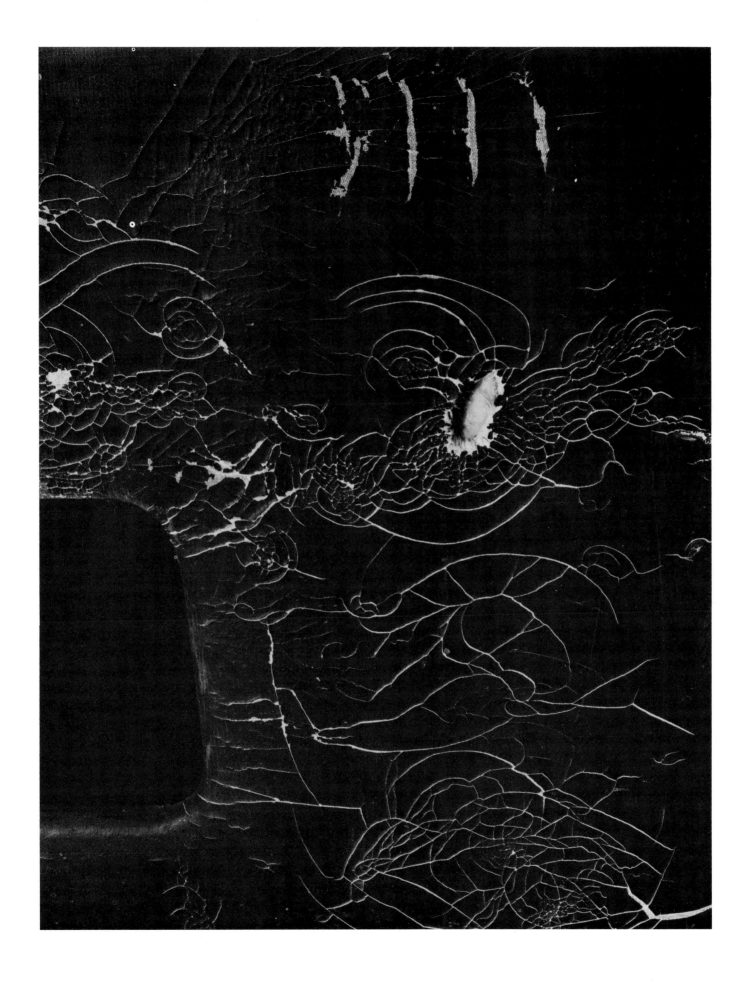

the road, and on the dry lake we had the unsettling experience of being completely surrounded by mirages. At one moment airy cliffs walled us in, at the next they dissolved into curtains of shimmering color beyond which no object could be distinguished. The wavering light world suddenly vanished and Amboy lay before us: a cluster of dilapidated shacks, one with its roof blown off, one with its backyard full of broken-down carnival wagons. Edward would have stopped for these except for the inevitable afternoon wind which was already carrying shingles and cans across the landscape.

The crater was a disappointment—just a big black hump—and the lava flow was so mixed with sand dunes as to be almost indistinguishable. It was a wilting afternoon, the wind was furnace-hot, and for miles around there was no patch of shade. We sucked the juice from grapefruit—even that was hot—and the water in the canteens tasted like cheap paint. Edward examined me suspiciously, said I was turning into a regular Curry, and that henceforward all suggestions relating to buttes or craters were to be regarded with deep distrust. On the long pull back to Twentynine Palms I consulted the map that had led me astray. The only trouble with it, and all other Southern California Auto Club maps, was that it was too good. Every desert pack trail was laid out clear as a highway; each abandoned soft drink stand appeared as a town. But I had added the mileage to Amboy and back as something over sixty miles; a more careful review of the figures brought the total to something over a hundred miles. There began my education in the art of map-reading.

We found a camping place south of Twentynine Palms just as darkness closed in. Edward had made but two negatives so there was no need to load, and after a supper enlivened with fresh avocados we lay back against our rolled-up sleeping bags, stretched our feet to the fire, and lolled in indolent ease. We had learned on the first trip that cigarettes were a waste of effort in the desert wind which burned them to the butt before you could get two puffs, that is, if you succeeded in lighting them at all. This trip we equipped ourselves with pipes. I had been presented with a fine curved-stem affair and a small can of imported tobacco. The latter now being exhausted, I dipped for the first time into the common hoard of Sontag Mixture. I almost decided smoking was a bad habit that should be given up.

Next morning we reached what the map, without exaggerating, called the WONDERLAND OF ROCKS. Here was desert granite to put both Deadmans Point and Rattlesnake Valley to shame: the piled-up boulders were no longer an isolated phenomenon, they were the very bones of the landscape. There were high carved walls of granite, wide smooth floors of granite, bulging hills and mountains of granite. Sensing an opportunity to show off my scanty desert lore I stated casually that granite tended to round itself off, and this explained all the big boulders balanced on top of smaller ones; that it was at heart the same stuff as the grey granite of the mountains—in fact, this was the remnant of an ancient mountain range; that its reddish yellow color—the product of sun and wind polish—was familiarly referred to as *desert glaze*. But Brett and Edward were too engrossed with the delights of the landscape to pay me heed; I am afraid if you asked them today what *desert glaze* is, they would have to shake their heads in embarrassed ignorance.

There was so much to photograph that our progress was slow. After a half-hour stop, we would meet at the car. Edward would say, "I'm all through here, how about you?" and Brett would say, "Sure. Let's move on." Cameras would be packed into the car, we would drive for perhaps three minutes, then Edward would say, "Wait a minute! I've got to take a look at this!" He would take his look, come back saying almost apologetically, "I'm afraid I'll have to do it." Out would come the cameras, one rock or Joshua would lead to another, and half an hour later the performance would be repeated. Five hours from breakfast we were not yet five miles from it.

I should explain here that I use "breakfast" to designate the first of the morning's repasts: fruit, or fruit juice, and coffee. During the day we had no regular meals. On top of the back-seat load we kept a food-box containing a variety of crackers, dried fruits, cheese, nut butters, and jam. If we had recently passed a store, there would be fresh fruit, lettuce, and milk; if not, there were cans of fruit, asparagus, sardines, etc., to vary the basic menu. When the need arose—and it did with amazing frequency—we would repair to the food-box singly, or together. Our appetites were so violent that we seldom dared to stray twenty steps from Heimy without first filling our pockets with dried fruit against a sudden seizure.

About noon we gathered at the car, disposed of a can of pineapple, and held council on the water problem. There was easily another day's work here but there wasn't another day's water, and we had to have a good supply for crossing the Pinto Basin on our way to Mecca. Here and there *tanks* were marked on the map, but when these open reservoirs in the rocks were not dry, the little rainwater they contained was brackish. Eight miles to the south the map said Lost Horse Well. That sounded like water and we decided to chance it.

Around the first turn we came upon a little yellow box of a house. A man clad in dirty jeans and a greasy hat, his cheeks covered with grey-white stubble, came out to meet us. Edward hailed him with an impulsive comment on the setting, "What a place to live, among these magnificent rocks!" The man looked carefully at Edward, suspecting he hadn't heard right, sent a brief glance to the clustered boulders that towered above us and said feelingly, "I guess you wouldn't think so if you'd lived here as long as I have."

Tobacco and spirits had played havoc with his vocal equipment, but he was ruthlessly eager to use it. Long solitude had slowed down his conversational faculties, his ideas were formed and delivered at snail pace, yet when we finally wrenched ourselves away we had learned that: his name was Jack, he'd lived there ten years, he was seventy-four years old, and we could always get water down at Lost Horse Well. Along with this information we had been favored with volumes of desert scandal concerning the Lost Horse people and their gold mines. So it was no surprise when the young man at Lost Horse Well, on being advised that the man up the road had directed us, responded thus, "Oh. [Silence] You mean old Jack. [Sustained silence] Yes, you can always get water here."

Driving back toward Jack's place we tried to decide what deeds could be villainous enough to kindle and perpetuate a feud between two parties living on an otherwise neighborless desert. We had reached no satisfactory conclusion when Edward arrested the discussion and Heimy with a vehement "*Stop!*" Five yards off our starboard bow stood a wholly unbelievable yucca. Two stalks rose from a base of bristling sword points: one, a swelling, intricately wrapped, green bud; the other, a spike of abundant greenish-yellow blossoms. Not yet at its majority, the flower stalk already stood seven feet high. So heavy-laden was each separate blossom stem that the faintest stirring of the air set the whole fragrant tower in trembling motion.

No pushing on across the desert then. Nothing would do but we must camp on the spot so Edward could exploit his find in morning light. Meanwhile there were plenty of spectacular rock piles in the vicinity to keep both photographers occupied. Having found a suitable campsite—a clearing free from cactus and anthills, with a face of rock at one side to build our fire against, a detached uninteresting rock that no one would want to photograph—I set about my third repair job. During these last warm days I had discarded my boots in favor of alpargatas, only to find that such comfortable footwear could not long survive constant contact with granite surfaces. The rope soles had frayed out, retaining only the most superficial connection with the canvas tops. Hoping to extract a few more days' service, I bound them from instep to toe with strips of cotton sheeting.

Coffee was made with caution that night and ablutions were of the most casual. We had sixty miles of desert to cross before our canteens would be refilled, perhaps another day's photography before even that crossing began. But water conservation had already become a habit. We had learned that even in the heat of the day one mouthful of water is sufficient to assuage thirst for some time; also that one stays remarkably clean in the desert. How people lived on the desert before paper towels, I can't guess. We used them for everything, but especially in dishwashing.

Jack's house was but a stone's throw from our camp, so next morning while Edward hovered over his prize, I decided to do some social research in feudin'. The old man had clung to us with such tenacity the day before, I was taken aback to see he didn't recognize me. He explained by drawing off the greasy hat and exhibiting a hole in his head the size of a fist. Followed a long narration about how there was some dynamitin' goin' on up in San' Marg'rita Canyon, an' a spinnin' rock hit him, an' he fell on the only ledge in the whole canyon, an' the doctor at the hospital said it was a triple compounded frackshure, but he wouldn't let them keep him in bed six months, no sir, he got up and walked around all he pleased, and anyhow sometimes his memory don't work quite so good.

Edward had advised me to fill my pouch and offer him some tobacco but Jack turned it down, and interrupted himself every ten words to say by god he'd seen some queer ones in his time but I was the first wommin he ever saw smokin' a pipe. Then, probably to warn me in good time: "Ye know a man gits to smokin' pipe tobaccah, an' he's got to have a stronger kind and a stronger kind, and purty soon he's got the strongest kind they is an' it still aint strong enough."

To lead up diplomatically to my real interest I said, "They have a nice place at Lost Horse Well." This provoked a snort of derision and a storm of malicious comment on the personalities and private lives of Them People. When at last I stemmed the tide, I gave up diplomacy, and proceeded by direct question. Jack's version of the feud: They wanted him to take care of their place while they were away and he refused. Next time they drove into town they didn't stop for him and didn't bring back his mail. Next time they did stop, and he told them there was the road and to keep a-goin' and never set foot on his place again. This last, delivered with reminiscent relish, was followed by a full minute of hoarse chuckles and emphatic leg-slapping.

Then he got to the subject that really interested him. I was conducted through the catalogue of all the feminine visitors he had ever had, what they'd said to him, what he'd said to them, and how they drank. "So she said, Jack, she said, you know you've never seen me intoxicated, and I said, [chuckle] well, now maybe not what you'd rightly call intoxicated, I said, but I seen that look in your eye, I said . . . ." When I rose to depart he ambled outside with me and bemoaned the fact that he had to climb up on the roof to fix the chimney—like as not he'd fall off like he did the last time.

Good-bye to the rocks, then. Edward has his fill and so has Brett. Pack up the cameras. "No, just a moment. Let's look at this one over here; a bulging boulder, cleft through the center, cross furrowed with geometrical precision—and, yes, that one across there, with the light striking its pitted wind-scoured surface and the tidy little round bushes clinging in the cracks—and, oh yes, look! Here's a monumental one with carved columns—and here—" but at last we did tear ourselves away to roll south between the mountains down into the Pinto Basin.

That was a road indeed! It was made of giant corduroy. The cross ridges were one or two feet high and they were spaced at intervals a little shorter than the length of the car and they went on forever. Heimy limped over the humps; we sweated and groaned because there was nothing to look at but greasewood, and some nicely colored distant mountains—the Pintos—which Edward would surely have looked at if we had not been to Death Valley. That went on for hours. Then there was a sandy river bed surrounded by a whole forest of smoke trees and Edward went in with his camera and came out saying "I made one, but I don't know why, because I don't like it." So I pulled out the index and entered, "April 30. Nr. Pinto Basin. *Smoke Trees.* (Don't know why.) Neg. 39."

Suddenly there was a lot of bright blue ahead, the Salton Sea, and here were Mecca and fresh cool water. We doused our heads and let the water drip down our shirts and for all of three minutes felt wonderfully cool. Then there was the good-smelling general store, with the shoes opposite the bananas, but the clerk said "No, we don't bother to stock dates; roadside stands do all the business. Where is the nearest? Around the turn and across the tracks."

The trim building was of the Hollywood bungalow persuasion; because it had a certain air about it, we sought confidence by attacking in force. Brett and Edward with four days' worth of beard apiece, stamping their dusty boots; Brett's pants bandanna-patched, Edward's adhesive-taped; I, in comparatively flawless shirt and pants, but with alpargatas sheet-wound, trailing little shreds of rope, complete the picture by gnawing an apple—thus we entered the sacred precincts of a date temple. The spotless showcases held a smattering of dates; here and there about the room small boxes of dates, wrapped in colored cellophane, were displayed singly on elegant pedestals.

A young goddess tiptoed into the hushed apartment, asked in little more than a whisper what was desired. At this moment a really superb Russian wolfhound appeared in another doorway and I made a friendly gesture to it. The hound put one dainty foot forward. "Duchess!" came withering rebuke from the goddess. Then to

CALIFORNIA AND THE WEST

me with studied disapproval: "Would you please go over to the door if you want to pet her? We don't like to have her in the showroom." No rapid deductions were necessary to assure me that Duchess, every hair meticulously in place, was far more eligible for the showroom than certain parties whose outlandish costumes were at that moment reflected in the polished tile floor. I nodded silent farewell to her elegance and withdrew, soon followed by two disgusted males. They carried a tiny packet containing perhaps fifteen dates, price twenty-five cents. We had omitted dates from the supply list this trip purposely, in order to get them here in their home territory. Now we were washed clean of our last shreds of travel-innocence.

The sun was on the afternoon side but still glaring hot when we turned up into the range of mud-hills north of the Sea and entered Painted Canyon. We drove up the gravelly stream bed between sheer cliffs of colored clay several hundred feet high. At times the walls closed in so Heimy could barely squeeze between them. There was no sunlight in these narrow defiles, only a gloomy twilight of underwater green. In a branch canyon we discovered an island of sandy soil supporting a half dozen mesquites, and settled on it for a campsite.

We were preparing the evening stew when a shrill persistent squeaking drew our attention to a crack in the pink and yellow wall behind us. It was a narrow slit, about three feet long, and a dozen feet above our heads. We waited in silence, craning our necks. For several minutes nothing appeared, then little grey bundles began to drop out, catch their wings, and flicker away in the dusk. There must have been a good-sized cave within, for thousands of bats came out while we watched. They tumbled out in groups of thirty or forty, then there would be a pause while a new set moved up to the entrance; all the time the chorus of squeaks maintained a steady accompaniment. We had finished our coffee and were at work on our evening pipes before the last flight was launched and silence settled down on the canyon. Next morning when dawn-light began to pale the moon and stars, they came silently gliding back to re-enter skillfully their secret cliff dwelling.

Photography is a stern business after all. We cannot stay in these cool dim aisles of twilight because climate and subject matter refuse to be together at their best. We must go out and crawl across the barren sun-scorched plain, down the east side of the Salton Sea; we must swelter through the desert-reclaimed Imperial Valley—a paradise of cantaloupes, etc., to be sure, but a climate no human being should be asked to endure. Around the south end of the sea, then turn up the west side and start to look for sandstone concretions. A friend had brought some to Edward several years before: strangely formed yellow stones, like twined snakes, in intricate patterns of circles and ovals.

54

A little gas station appeared on the grey flatness with a yard full of what we wanted.

"We like these things. Where do you get them?"

"I dunno. I dunno where they come from. Man just brings 'em to me."

"Oh. We thought they came from around here."

"Nope. I dunno. Man just brings 'em from somewheres else."

Shimmering heat waves on the grey flat world. Scorching, sun-baked desolation. No foreground, distance, or horizon. No boulder, tree, or object. Oh yes, there was something square sticking up—a sign. SANDY BEACH: *Boat Races, January 22, 23, 24, 25.* Were we months or years late for the sporting event? What did it matter; Sandy Beach sounded like Pearly Gates, and we bounded off on the dirt road leading seaward. In a minute every one was yelling at once, "Look!" "Look over here!" "There they are!" pointing to concretions that were suddenly all around us. It was only a scattered batch of very small ones but our faith was renewed.

Of course, it wasn't a sandy beach, that would be too much to expect. Instead the footing was over a salt-crusted expanse of sodden mud. Four battered, diminutive bathhouses were perched on the higher ground; over at the end of the mud strip there was a dismal clump of decaying palms dipping sad fronds in the sea. The water was warm as restaurant soup until we were in up to the waist, then the feet encountered a substratum of icy cold. We lay in the water like fixed buoys, without energy to move or swim.

Then, restored in spirit, we moved north up the main road. Soon we learned to spot dull veins of orange, crossing the grey and tan landscape, that marked rich deposits of concretions. A maze of wheel tracks led off seaward, where the far distance showed some tiny spots of green. Heimy twisted between little arroyos and over hummocks, crossed broken pavements of concretions, arrived at the green: a few stunted mesquites on the bank of a dry stream bed. While Brett and Edward drove off on a scouting trip, I made camp, which is to say I unrolled my sleeping bag and lay down on it. Never had we camped in such emptiness; there had always been a rock or a hill for security. Here there were only flat space and punishing heat, against which the spindly mesquites offered no defense.

The explorers returned and lined up their trophies against the stream bank. Sunset brought no relief from the heat. We couldn't face the thought of hot food so we swigged down some fruit juice, opened canned vegetables and ate them cold. At four next morning the air seemed no cooler than when we had gone to bed. Before we had finished our coffee there was a vicious red warning streak across the eastern sky.

We reduced our clothing to the legal minimum and set out with the tools of treasure hunting: sun helmets, cameras, the pint canteen—and a whiskbroom to dust off the ends of partially embedded concretions that needed moving. But landmarks were the vexing problem. Edward would mean to return to a particular place when the light was better, but the place would have disappeared: each dry wash was a duplicate of its neighbor and all the low scrubby bushes were identical. Presently I took inspiration and returned to camp for a roll of toilet paper: in no time fluttering white banners were attached to anonymous little bushes to mark concretion sites.

The concretions were heavy but fragile. Often they broke at a touch. The forms were amazingly beautiful and varied, and all through the morning gleeful shouts arose from the sun-baked wasteland as one or another announced discovery of a new and more exotic specimen. Brett's enthusiasm proved his undoing; he was running with a large concretion clasped to his chest when his foot encountered a chuckhole. In the subsequent crash he saved the concretion at the expense of a wrenched back.

By ten o'clock the sun's efforts, plus reflection from the baked ground, plus the complete absence of any shade or breeze, had dulled our appetite for treasure; we trudged back to camp with eyes front, ignoring the beckoning banners to right and left. By spreading our sleeping bag sheets over the mesquites we made a little patch of shade in the creek bed. Brett and I peeled off our clothes and lay there panting, while Edward proved his sturdier stock by tramping around for another hour in the blazing sun. He might have kept it up all afternoon, I think, but the black rubberized material of the focussing cloth began to fry the top of his head and the insides of the black camera cases heated up like ovens. So, towards noon, we packed up and headed back to the highway.

With windows open and windshield raised we bounded north along the straight road at fifty miles an hour, creating a soothing if temporary breeze. High on the hills to the west we could follow the markings of the ancient beach line, and wish—except for those concretions—that this whole scorched basin might return to its proper and prehistoric function as lake bottom. Now reappeared the sign series that had begun the day before: 28 MILES TO DATE MILKSHAKES, 25 MILES TO DATE MILKSHAKES, 18 MILES TO DATE MILKSHAKES. Our first mild curiosity was whipped to fever-pitch as the miles grew fewer and the utterly impossible-sounding beverage came closer.

Any last misgivings retained from our recent date debacle were melted away on sight of the open-front stand, curtained with masses of blooming flowers, its shady recesses enhanced by the activity of a large electric fan. Even after all that build-up, I have to admit there is no way to describe date milkshakes; they must be tasted to be understood. They bear no relationship to the syrupy, straw-clogging mass commonly associated with the term milkshake. They are not too rich, not too sweet; and as I say, there is no word for what they are—they are perfectly constructed for desert consumption. We sat back dallying with our second round, deciding the rough life had its compensations, after all.

Then we crossed the highway to see John Hilton, desert naturalist, to whom Hanna had given us a letter. We examined the stone house he had built himself, his collection of rare cacti, his family of desert tortoises, and settled down to talk about concretions. Hilton told us this area had been a river bed more anciently than it had been a lake bed; that calcite trying to crystallize in the mud of the river bed had made the concretions. He showed us two little ones in which the crystallization process had kept to more conventional lines, producing triangle and diamond shapes rather than circles and ovals. He shared our enthusiasm for their beautiful forms, told us he had once whitewashed a particularly good one and exhibited it to friends as the work of a newly discovered modern sculptor. The beholders had clamored for more of the artist's work. We asked about the mazes of wheel-tracks winding over the concretion terrain, and he told us the stones were hauled away by the truckload to be sold at fancy prices for Beverly Hills rock gardens.

Being assured we were here to photograph, not depredate, he agreed to guide us to a virgin field, known only to himself, which contained more and finer concretions than the whole sea-margin we had been exploring. We decided to make this treasure field our night's camp and set out with a detailed map. Yes, here was the proper arroyo. Turn down under the bridge, and wind up the river bed. Now watch for the landmarks: a spring, a palm, a V-division in the course, a grove of smoke trees, another palm. We never found any of them. If we saw a palm, it was on the wrong side of the wash; if there was a V-division, only one branch was wide enough for Heimy and that was the wrong one. The banks rose higher, the channel narrowed, more and bigger rocks littered the right of way. We had driven twelve miles up the river and darkness was coming fast.

Well, here was a low clay shelf projecting into the river bed, one end sloped so Heimy could climb onto it, a small flat for the sleeping bags. It shouldn't rain at this time of year, but if it did we'd be safe up to a three-foot rise. But instead of a river a hot wind came roaring downstream. We ate more cold vegetables and drank fruit juice. Brett's back was aching severely. Edward nearly perished loading in the car. Even outside, the air was suffocating and the furnace blast poured down on us all night long.

By morning Brett's back was so bad we must head for home. Going down wash we stopped now and then, climbed the thirty-foot banks, looked around on top for concretions. On the try we agreed should be the last, Edward found some—not Hilton's—and hauled the camera up. These were embedded ones, small flat slabs set in the clay like tiles in relief. But, with the bellows extended all the way and the camera pointed straight down, how was Edward ever to get high enough to see into the ground glass? We dragged up flat concretion slabs, stacked them in a teetery pile; precariously balanced on top, Edward made three negatives.

Oh, the insidious advertisers! Who could go by all those signs and resist? Of course, we stop for date milkshakes again. Then up through the palm groves where advertising is carried far past reason. Sample: *Special Dates—5c apiece—Only One to a Visitor*. The billboards threaten and cajole but, safely full of date milkshakes, we are immune. Up the southern end of the San Jacintos, the rocky slope speckled with cacti and yuccas and old agave stalks set in the dark shale; Edward keeps watching for the right place but before he finds it we are up in oaks and piñons. Then real pine forest with birds and squirrels and grassy meadows, where Edward makes some negatives of bark patterns on a burned pine.

In Hemet we invade the grocery for lettuce and celery and anything green and crunchy. The clerk runs a practiced eye over our haberdashery and queries without much question, "You guys been fishin'?" And not long after we are on Foothill Boulevard, nearing Los Angeles, buying all the dates we can eat at fifteen cents a pound.

3 Colorado Desert

The Old Butterfield Stage Route

THE second trip's negatives were developed and in storage. Edward's camera cases were coated with chaste white paint. He had an elegant new focussing cloth—a four-by five-foot rectangle of sateen, two layers of black and a top layer of white. (I worried him by saying I could use it between trips for an evening wrap.) Now it was the middle of May, Los Angeles was sweltering in a heat wave, and we were debating: should we risk the third desert route this late or put it off until fall? We drove to the drugstore; Edward went in to telephone and came back to the car looking baffled.

"Well, what did Hanna say?"

"He said it might be a little warmish."

We looked hopefully at each other, studying over the words to find if some meaning could possibly be extracted.

"It couldn't be worse than this," Edward began cautiously.

I pulled out the route map for the fifteenth time that day and looked again at the red loop that curled down almost to the Mexican border. "There are some mountains handy. Six thousand feet up, with lakes. If it got too bad we could go up there and cool off."

We sat back and looked around us at the sizzling streets, the drooping populace. Edward said, "Let's go shop," and at those words Heimy, who already preferred rough roads and solitude to smooth ones and traffic, leaped forward with a whine of pleasure.

Getting out of Los Angeles in any direction is dull driving; whoever called it Seven Suburbs in Search of a City used poetic license in grossly underestimating the number of searchers. Finally, we left them behind and headed southward down the middle of the coast range.

Orange groves, terraced hills, oil derricks, to Annaheim; through a green river canyon to Corona whose every other building is a church; through fertile valleys and rolling hills, red cattle dreaming in the high green grass; past Lake Elsinore, its blue surface hidden by the tight-wedged shoreline of beach clubs, yacht clubs, hotels, and inns; between waving fields of barley and wheat; around the marshy rim of Lake Henshaw; down a shady canyon of live oaks and pines.

The miles of pastoral landscape under hot blue skies made us drowsy and we pulled up at the roadside to eat and nap. "Where are we going to camp tonight?" "This canyon looks nice and cool." But every other tree had a sign on it. PROPERTY OF SAN DIEGO WATER COMPANY. NO CAMPING. NO HUNTING. NO SHOOTING. NO FIRES. NO TRESPASSING. FINES. IMPRISONMENT, etc. So we climbed up the mountain to Julian, an old mining town now domesticated with fields and orchards, its frame buildings half hidden by creamy billows of locust blossoms. Then slid down the other side by the steep Z-course of the Banner grade, through a narrow green-shadowed ravine that emptied us into the San Felipe Valley. We must find the Scissors Crossing, a couple of narrow branch roads hidden in the sea of low brush. We were now on a section of the old Butterfield Stage Route that we would follow fifty-six miles across the desert to the southern highway (US 80: San Diego-Yuma). Map search revealed a little dry lake some miles along at the southern end of the valley; an arrow pointing past it was labelled PAINTED ROCKS. That sounded like a camping place.

The now familiar—from Death Valley and Pinto Basin—red-and-white auto-club sign appeared:

WARNING

DO NOT ATTEMPT

THIS ROUTE

WITHOUT

AMPLE SUPPLIES

OF WATER

GAS * OIL

and soon after it yuccas, ocotillos, and chollas. Presently the road climbed a low hill and we looked down on a desert Eden. Cupped between dry rocky ridges lay a little vale carpeted with grass and edged by a half dozen fat shade trees. It took us several minutes to be convinced this was indeed the dry lake. There was a cactus-less gravel flat against the ridge for our campsite and all the flowers that ever grew on a desert bloomed around it.

The sun was still above the western mountain rim, so off to hunt painted rocks. Heimy pitched and tossed on the bumpy trail, plunged into a thicket of tall shrubs whose branches, massed with butter-yellow blossoms, reached well above his head. I climbed out to investigate and had to eat a lot of harsh words; the magnificent yellow forest was nothing but the hitherto much abused greasewood. The galloping track led to no Painted Rocks that we could find but it wound around the base of a hill criss-crossed with live and dead agave stalks, standing, fallen, tipping at every angle. Edward eyed them with longing but the sun was going fast; they must wait for morning. Back through the yellow forest to our enchanted camp to watch the orange sunset-light climb up the cactus-studded hill behind us.

The air was blandly warm and still and full of flower scents. A banquet was in order, and out of a mysterious birthday box it came: stuffed olives, pickled onions, antipasto, camembert cheese, marinated herring, and a whole salami! Too warm for a fire, so half a moon came up to light the feast while a cricket chorus provided incidental music. We made an extra pot of coffee and filled the thermos for an early morning start, then lay on our sleeping bags watching the moonlight wash over the landscape, dropping neat pools of inky shadow under the trees.

At dawn the air was still warm—the thermos coffee cold. No matter; we drank it that way, and dashed off for negatives of the agave-stalked hill in sunrise light. All morning we moved slowly south. Edward found so much to look at that Heimy must be held to a dawdling walk so nothing would be missed. There were junipers with their berries out, *yucca mojavensis*, Spanish bayonets, agaves, and every kind of cactus. The sky was a brilliant cloudless blue, the air motionless, the silence perfect.

From the top of a grade called La Puerta we looked down on the supreme redundancy, Vallecitos Valley. The Vallecito stage station is admirably restored (how nice if the same restraint governed mission restorations): more or less square rooms opening into one another, dirt floors, thick walls, small windows. So cool inside we might stay all day, but the sign on the door says not to camp in the building. The thatch of the roof is lashed to poles with strips of cowhide; from nests under the eave long streamers of birdlime run down the wall—tempting Edward to a negative.

In front of the station are trees and a patch of green tules where clear water runs out of a little pipe. We lunched there in the shade, filled ourselves and canteens at the spring, and took up our southward way. So far the road had been good, for the benefit of Vallecito visitors; but here it gave up all pretense and settled into a sandy river bed. We had met two cars in the course of the morning; now we realized they must have camped at the station for there were no fresh tire-tracks on the sand before us.

Edward made negatives of ocotillos and chollas that appeared on the banks; when we stopped I left Heimy in midstream since there was no way to turn out without miring in deep sand, and there were no cars to turn out for. A silent empty landscape, not even a lizard astir. Once in a while a buzzard sailed slowly overhead. The heat became more intense as the day wore on, and we had more frequent recourse to the canteen. We stopped to eat and discovered convincingly that this was the hottest day we had yet experienced: the cocoanut butter was melted to milk and the jack cheese ran like cream soup.

We had discarded most of our clothing by two o'clock, and by three had accounted for a gallon of water apiece. The dry heat was not unbearable, but the blinding glare of the white sand was hard on the eyes. We came out of the wash into a wide flat bowl between the mountains, and the wheel-tracks that had so far exhibited singleness of purpose began to branch off in all directions. No signposts, of course. We selected the deepest ruts at each division and trusted to luck. When salt crust appeared on the road, willows beside it, and grass, we were reassured; the second station is called Carrizo and that means reed grass, so we felt we must be right.

Animals at last, big lumbering jack rabbits ambling in and out of the bushes, showing no fear, only mild interest in our presence. We had passed items of dead cattle for some time and now Edward found a beautiful set of half-picked cow bones gleaming in the marsh grass. Interrupted buzzards arose from near-by prizes and circled above us while he made a negative. We plowed on through deepening sand and came to our first road-sign in hours. It was pointing askew but there was only one side trail; we rolled forward to the magic music of running water and the astonishing sight of a slender cottonwood and a eucalyptus, planted long since on the stream bank.

Carrizo creek usually keeps underground, but here it was out on top, wide, shallow, and cheerful. A pile of crumbling adobe bricks and a grave were all that marked the site of the stage station. Back at the road junction we made a discovery over-looked in our excitement at nearing real water and trees. A few stones and pieces of broken bottle were set in a barricade across the main trail; in the middle a wooden cross was stuck in the sand, a scrap of cardboard with pencilled writing on it fixed to the crossbar.

Carrizo May 17 37
Please help sick man at Carrizo Station
Resp Geo T Edwards

Today was May 17th; we had just been to Carrizo and seen no one. We dug up a ton of sand getting Heimy reversed in the narrow trail and drove slowly back to the creek. We hallooed, but no answer. Faint wheel-tracks wandered off this way and that; we circled around, calling, looking, listening. We had given up and started back to the road, when we passed the cottonwood and eucalyptus; Edward saw the feet sticking out and said, "There he is."

He lay on his back between the trees, half on a light piece of tarpaulin; a short, emaciated man with close-cropped hair and a stubble of red beard. His faded blue jacket and once-white shirt were open across his chest; his worn corduroy pants were ripped and roughly mended; long underwear showed under the torn cuffs. One battered shoe was off, lying near the small bare foot. His open eyes stared straight up. One hand rested lightly on his chest, the other lay at his side with the thumb and middle finger pressed together. Beside him stood a half-full bottle of fresh milk, a can of water with KY stamped on it, and a small bundle done up in a blue bandanna with a pencil through the knot.

We stood a long while looking at him, only the creek running below us making a soft sound in the hot silence of the desert afternoon. I had never seen a dead person, and had supposed it would somehow shock or upset me. And since we had seen buzzards circling up the creek, I had been preparing myself for the kind of thing the books describe when a man goes crazy of thirst, tears off his clothes, hurls himself on the ground grasping for mirages, and finishes, an unspeakable sight. But this man had died so quietly and easily it was hard to convince myself he was really dead; I kept expecting to see his chest rise and fall in gentle breathing.

Edward took a full-length picture of the man, just as he lay with the articles around him, then climbed through the brush behind the eucalyptus to photograph the head. Meanwhile I opened the bandanna to see what we could learn. On top in the bundle were two imitation banknotes with $100 marks on the four corners, an advertisement for THE LOCAL LOAN COMPANY in the center. On one he had written in pencil, "I pick this up in the road. No good." On the other, "This coupon no good." In a wandering hand on these and another scrap of paper: "Please tell my people," and a name and address in Tennessee. Then came a bundle of about fifty Alpine Milk coupons, a rag stuck full of sewing implements, and a Minnie Mouse spoon. Then a separate little cloth bag of rolled oats, and inside that, carefully wrapped in a bit of newspaper and tied with string, a fishhook.

I copied the name and address of his people, put the bundle together and retied it, remembering that if you saved a great many Alpine Milk coupons you could get a silver-plated spoon, and wondering if he would have discarded Minnie Mouse when he got it or kept them both. It had been all right at first, I had felt impersonal about it. But now that I had pried into his worldly possessions and seen the spoon, the banknotes that were "no good," and the fishhook, he seemed so small and shrunken and lonely I couldn't just stand there looking at him. I went around the tree to see how Edward was getting on.

A thick pile of brush on the stream bank put the head and arm in deep shadow. Edward had just finished saying he had to make a negative as a record, in spite of the shade, when a little sun cut through the branches lighting the face.

The sun was getting low when we covered the dead man over with his tarpaulin and returned to the main trail. The greenery dropped behind as we followed the Carrizo wash down between the Coyote and the Fish Creek Mountains. There was no after-glow of soft sunset colors that evening; daylight departed swiftly and completely and in its place came an ominous grey twilight, with a hot wind roaring down at our back, spraying Heimy with pebbles. A remarkably sheltered campsite should have turned up then, but it didn't. The sand and gravel wash spread away flat and forbidding. Even the greasewood grew in stunted foot-high bushes, and the road was cut with cross-washes that put the Pinto Basin road to shame. Occasionally these would be varied by areas of low badlands where the trail would climb straight up a little ridge and drop off so suddenly that nothing save the distant hills would be visible over the hood. Then I would hold Heimy poised on the brink while Edward got out to see which way the road went down.

The blowing sand was problem enough while daylight lasted, but when full darkness came it was worse. An opaque grey curtain hung always before us, impene-trable to the headlights. When we could see fifteen feet of the road ahead visibility was good. We jolted along at five miles an hour, sometimes leaving the trail to avoid the deepest gouges, usually crashing into one while avoiding another. The desert was show-ing us what it could do and we were impressed. Edward has never learned to drive, what with four boys to do it for him, and despite a year of high-school physics my motor-knowledge ends at the dashboard. Heimy was a new car, not yet subject to most of the ills the secondhands are heir to, but he had not been put together with this kind of roadbed in view.

So we considered all the rules we should follow, in case. How you conserve energy and water by finding a bit of shade and staying quiet during the heat of the day. Then at night you start walking by the stars. It was, of course, absurd. No human being could have followed the trail, let alone the stars, on a night like this. He would have all he could do to stand upright and keep his eyes open in the torrent of blowing sand. But it was comforting to think we knew the right thing to do even if it wouldn't work.

Mostly we occupied ourselves with the man at Carrizo. From the Tennessee address and the KY water can we decided he had just come out from the south and didn't know what a California desert was. Probably expected to find avocados and oranges and dates growing all over the place. Perhaps he had been at Carrizo several days. George T. Edwards must have been on foot, maybe taking cattle or sheep through, maybe prospecting. At any rate, he couldn't do anything for the sick man beyond leaving the milk and the sign in the road. And if he had the date right, the man was probably already too far gone for help.

We had seen no cars since we left Vallecito; this was clearly not a popular road. But then, perhaps we were no longer on the road? With so many unmarked branchings we might long ago have left the proper course. The map said eighteen miles from Carrizo to the highway and we had been going on this way for more than three hours. My eyes had ached all day from the glare, and now as I tried to see through the grey billows of blowing sand, I could feel a hundred separate particles of sand gently cruising the surface of my eyeballs. Suddenly a strange dark line appeared slashed across the sand ahead of us—and another. The headlights hit them and reflected back; a railroad track! We bounced down a gully, jolted up the other side, and saw giant fireflies moving in the distance—headlights on the highway.

Oh, the heavenly floating sensation of those nine smooth miles to El Centro. No shopping around for accommodations. We turned into the first place we saw, the City Limit Tourist Camp, and asked the proprietor to call the sheriff while we unloaded our duffel. The cabin walls were screened halfway down so the least stirring of air rustled the white curtains, providing a pleasant illusion of coolness. We tottered into the kitchen, turned on the faucet, and stood watching the absorbing spectacle of running water. We washed our hands and faces, doused our heads, splashing the stuff around recklessly.

We were reclining on the creaky bed drinking lukewarm tomato juice when the sheriff appeared. With difficulty I avoided staring at him because he looked exactly like all the sheriffs in all the Western movies I had ever seen. When we had given him the Edwards message and the Tennessee address and told him what there was to tell, he said with obvious relief that this being Imperial County, and Carrizo being just over the line, the San Diego County sheriff would get the job. He went away to telephone, came back in half an hour as we sat listlessly eating a cold dinner, to ask if there had been any animal tracks around. It had occurred to him the man might have been a prospector. We said no, no animal tracks, and told him our theory.

He told us often weeks passed without a single car crossing that stretch, that temperatures of 120° were not uncommon, that on the average one person died out there every year. By this time I was beginning to think I had been pretty smart to keep on the right road, so I asked him about all the unmarked branchings; he said it wouldn't matter which you took, they were just alternates made when the trail was wet or to avoid chuckholes, etc., and they all rejoined the main trail sooner or later. Then he regaled us with a few stories of desert travelers dying of thirst, and one about a dried-up cow they propped between two ocotillos where it stood three years with the skin intact.

My eyes felt like live coals by now and my head was splitting. Edward decided to save trouble in loading by blacking out the kitchen. We nailed blankets over the windows but too much light came through, so Edward put a blanket over the kitchen table and sat on the floor underneath it. I was just dozing off in the next room when the door flew open and Edward emerged stripped to his shorts and looking as though he had just stepped out of a shower. Sweat had been running into his eyes and off the end of his nose, likely as not onto the films; unloading was finished, but loading yet to do. Thereupon we performed the comparatively simple maneuver of shrouding Heimy in the tarpaulin; it was midnight before we got to bed.

A sink to wash in, a chair to sit on, coffee at a table. No use going anywhere in a hurry with all the comforts of home here and paid for. We dawdled over coffee, Edward wrote postcards, I brought the log up to date, we swept out the car. The morning was half gone before we pulled out of the City Limit and set Heimy's nose to the west towards Yuha Plain.

From El Centro US 80 runs west over a desert so empty that even the resourceful Southern California Auto Club maps have to leave it blank white. A few wind-battered shacks stand forsaken at the roadside, their windows boarded up, gas pumps padlocked, waiting dismally for owners who will not return. About this Yuha Plain: Hanna had said we would find lots of concretions there. It was already apparent we would find plenty of heat. Our road didn't turn up all at once, but an hour's careful searching showed it could be only one thing: a mass of buckled and tilted blocks of oiled surface, half hidden by drifted sand, that wandered off to the south. Heimy plunged and lurched along it for a quarter mile to emerge on a barren plateau of baked clay that wavered in shimmering heat waves off to the horizon.

We followed the trail over little hummocks and gullies. Patches of ground were covered with desert pavement—small rocks bedded down by wind and water action to form a smooth mosaic flooring. This we had seen on the Mojave several times and up to now I had found it a charming desert phenomenon, especially since it always provided an admirable driving surface if we wished to forsake the road. But here it only seemed to accent the flat monotony of wasteland where all things must be levelled to the absolute horizontal or perish. Five miles of arid sameness, breezeless heat, and glaring ground. Then a few scattered concretions, weathered and broken, of no interest after the Salton Sea's rich harvest.

So back to the highway; on to the west, watching an army of dust devils sport over the plain. Edward photographed the warning sign and the twisty, but mild enough looking, beginning of the Carrizo road. He assured me he would be accused of symbolism because the shadow of the sign made a cross on the sand. (No one has noticed it yet.) An ideal country for getting all the sand you want. By now we had it in our hair and eyes and ears and between our teeth; sandstorms raged all around us. Hold on, there was a sign—PAINTED GORGE, 7 MILES—pointing off into the grey blow. A pox on Painted Gorge; we had had enough desert for the time being; we were going west till we found some mountains.

Here were the mountains and here was the road that went up to the lakes. But wait a minute! This was too much, even for California, the variety state: PUT ON YOUR CHAINS AND LOOK OUT FOR SNOW PLOW. Dazed but not entirely doubting, we asked at the gas station. No, there was no snow now, the sign was a leftover from winter. But up the road there were pines and oaks, green branches closing overhead, graciously cool air, shockingly green grass, diminutive streams splashing down the slopes.

We found an uninhabited campground on a hillside with a stream rushing by its base. Stone fireplaces with flat metal tops were set among the pines, there were wooden bench-and-table units, and, best of all, the clearings leveled for tents had been mattressed a foot deep with dry pine needles. Noisy black-crested jays and chattering squirrels surveyed our dinner preparations from overhead branches. Edward didn't have to load, but we could hardly go to bed at seven-thirty in such surroundings, so I decided to wash the cookset for a change. While the bucket of water heated, we broke out a pack of cigarettes for more variety, sat smoking and silently revelling in the smell of the pine woods, the noise of the brook, the white half-moon that climbed into the branches above us and made so much light we could have read a newspaper if we'd had one. When the cookset was washed and put away we could hold out no longer. We unrolled the sleeping bags on the pine-needle beautyrest and turned in at eight o'clock.

The Laguna Mountain Recreation Area—for that was what we were in—provided few negatives for Edward, but we had fallen in love with the green grass and trees and couldn't resist wandering all morning on the most unpromising roads. We climbed a wooden tower at the mountains' eastern edge and looked down an incredible distance on a tiny patch of green in a desert valley—Vallecito. It was already past believing that we had been there less than forty-eight hours before. The hardest blow was finding a signpost that pointed to Thing Valley, which we both agreed must be seen at all costs, only to discover the road's center ridge was too high for low-slung Heimy.

At noon we came out of the mountains to drive all day through the San Diego back country, choosing our roads haphazardly by whatever names appealed to us. We followed the Sweetwater River through a country of little ranches and orchards pocketed in miniature valleys between the dry hills. Once a bridge had been washed out and Heimy had his first swimming lesson. All day we saw fireplaces and chimneys, on lots beside new houses or in open fields. Edward kept watching for one to photograph while I kept trying to search out a great philosophical truth from the fact that when a house burns only that part which was meant for the fire remains.

We camped that night in Cuyamaca State Park, once more in the mountains with grass and trees and streams, and deer peering at us from the thickets. Acres of campsites to choose from, and not even a warden to collect fifty cents, because we were out of season. We chose a hilltop site, roofed with a spreading white oak; a big stack of cut wood by the fireplace, frogs singing down the hill, owls accompanying, moonlight bathing the slopes, heavenly coolness that called for extra blankets—for such a night we were determined to pay the state fifty cents, so we wasted an hour and a half next morning trying to track down a ranger who couldn't be found.

We went on back to base that day, hardly seeing tidy ranches, hills, and fields, after all that had gone before. But such a journey demanded a dramatic climax, and before we reached the coast, somewhere in the neighborhood of San Marcos, we found it. A battered, paint-peeled sign at the road's edge called our attention; we drove close to read:

GO SLOW
You are Now Entering
THE WINTERLESS GARDENS
Natural Habitat
of the Avocado

We went slow, through orchard after orchard of frost-blackened trees, a few brown leaves suspended from withered branches, here and there a shriveled lump that was once an avocado.

4 Desert and Coast

Farewell to the South

We returned to a dank and foggy Los Angeles to read garbled newspaper accounts of our desert adventure. In true journalese they had "propped" the dead man up against a "stunted tree" from which a faded bandanna had "fluttered." And, of course, he was "miles from water." The first day's developing discovered tragedy: a double exposure that lost the cow bones and the full-length of the dead man. We had known at the time that something was wrong—the total on my negative list had disagreed with the number of holders marked exposed—but what with the heat, being tired, general excitement, and any other possible excuse, we had miscalculated and Edward had repeated the wrong one.

Nor was that the only photographic tragedy. The films Edward had been using had caught an infectious skin disease: small transparent hyphens appeared in blank sky areas, ruining many of the best negatives. Edward was sure they were not his doing, and he finally secured an admission of factory fault, with assurance the trouble would be corrected at once.

We had completed Hanna's southern curriculum. His next route was a roundabout trip to San Francisco via, among other things, Yosemite Valley, Tioga Pass, Lake Tahoe. At this date Tioga Pass was still snowbound, so we decided to fill in with some short trips, beginning with Antelope Valley, a westerly projection of the Mojave, where Edward had made his first desert pictures twenty years before.

June fourth we set out with a friend, Zohmah Day. (Her parents named her Dorothy but at an early age she decided to make up her own name, settled on Zohmah, and managed to keep it.) We crossed the San Gabriels via Bouquet and San Francisquito Canyons in order to have a look at Elizabeth Lake, the subject (at sunset) of an early Weston. It was a pretty little blue pond with houses, trees, and picnic tables around it, and Edward strove unsuccessfully to find remembered landmarks.

An hour later, when we came down out of the mountains, I was even more forcefully reminded of all the good advice writers have given from time to time on not revisiting the scenes of your past. Where the desert should have been—where Edward, fresh from Chicago civilization, had first photographed Joshua trees and bleached cattle bones—a patchwork of tidy cultivated fields lay in a wide domestic panorama. Zohmah presented me with her own log of this trip; here it says: "Antelope Valley is now a reclaimed desert and Edward thought it a waste. He said wistfully, 'Let's go to the Wonderland of Rocks.'"

But instead we went to Red Rock Canyon. Here is Zohmah's reaction to life in the open:

We turned off the pavement up sideroads and around the cliffs and into side gullies, and got out of the car at every turn to test the wind that was blowing strong and gustily. No matter what angled rocks we got behind the wind came gushing in, too, so we settled on a place between blowings, unpacked food, stove, tarpaulin. . . . All that desert and cliff and sky going beyond where we sat and now the dark had come and blotted off the shape of the world, just space out there filled with things quite hidden and themselves. We had chosen a spot for ourselves, but maybe something in all that outdoors would come creeping, blowing in. . . . When they asked me to come on this trip, I knew I mustn't speak of how snakes frighten me, but couldn't help mentioning them conversationally. Charis said, "Sure, there are lots of them and especially at night." Edward said, "They won't bother you at all, but sleep in the middle and we will protect you."

The remark about snakes was meant for a joke—I didn't know till later how ill-timed. But if Zohmah was as frightened as she afterward led others to believe, she concealed it well. Next morning, in her honor I'm certain, since it was the only bit of unfriendly wildlife we saw in two years' travel, I found a baby scorpion crushed under my sleeping bag.

All morning we explored the side issues of Red Rock Canyon, Edward so delighted by the absence of wind that he found plenty to photograph. Cruising along the main highway through the canyon, we came upon a delightful witticism: a small, arrow-shaped sign pointing off into the desert where no road lay, saying, 190 MILES TO SULPHUR MINES. Then we set off to see a petrified forest recommended by a photographer friend. Up a well-graded one-way road, courtesy of Old Dutch Cleanser which has seismotectonic deposits here, through six miles of desert canyon, to pull up before a sign: PETRIFIED FOREST—*Guide 50c per person*. If the sign on the main road had contained that information we wouldn't have minded; but this was the great American gyp-game and we were resolved not to be taken.

A lanky individual lounged forth from the shack that stood in a semicircle of grey-white cliffs, to inform us we couldn't make the rounds without a guide. Edward flashed his press card—a handy weapon supplied by Hanna—and, when the guide still demurred, asked to see the owner. We waited wilting in the blazing sun until that gentleman arrived, booted, helmeted, sweating profusely. Edward explained himself, produced all his official documents; the owner, suitably impressed, waved the guide to take us around free.

Naturally, this gentleman, having watched the major portion of a dollar fifty slip from his grasp, was not in the best of humors. But his love of natural beauty undoubtedly conquered any baser feelings, for he set right to work to be helpful.

EDWARD *(to Zohmah and me):* "No use lugging the camera around in this heat. We'll take a look first and see what there is."

GUIDE: "Better take your camera right along with you. You'll find plenty of stuff to take."

EDWARD *(politely):* "I like to work slowly. I'd rather size up the material first, then get the camera if I need it."

GUIDE: "Well, that's the wrong way to do it here. The men from the *Times* and the *Examiner*, when they came here, they didn't waste any time at all. Just set down their cameras and bang, they had a picture."

EDWARD *(with increasing firmness):* "Very interesting, I'm sure. I still prefer to work slowly."

GUIDE: "Well, all I can say is you'll get much better results around here if you work fast: just set up and shoot the stuff is the only way. . . . "

The next speech had a certain rough authority; if the guide didn't confine his remarks to petrified wood thereafter, he at least abandoned the photography lesson. We trudged up the trail past little heaps of petrified limbs; at each disinterment the guide spat on a section and rubbed it with a grimy forefinger "to bring out the grain." He spoke with a good deal more enthusiasm of what was not yet uncovered, than of the surface displays. At the top of the hill he led us into a cave, pointed dramatically at the jagged outline of the entrance, and said, "See?" When we admitted we didn't, he explained delightedly, "Aimee's profile."

He told us "they" were going to build a mammoth resort hotel there, mostly underground. People would come on the main highway to the west, have a road to the top of the mountain, and be brought down this side in elevators. I have no idea how the subject of wolves came up but he was quick to assure us that California was still full of them—he had seen them not so far from that very spot. His best nature story was about the gila monsters, which also appeared to abound in this vicinity. He had seen them many's the time lie flat on the ground perfectly imitating the call of a crow until one of those unsuspecting birds was lured down—whereupon the clever lizard pounced on it and devoured it.

Edward found nothing to set up and bang away at, so we drove on back to Red Rock Canyon. Next morning, while Edward wandered around looking for the right rocks on which to photograph a preposterously curled-up high-heeled shoe we had found, I searched the maps for a new way back to town. I found one that crossed a couple of divides to join the Angels Crest Highway and come down Mt. Wilson. Aliso Canyon was full of tall Spanish bayonets blooming, but there was always just enough wind to discourage Edward from even setting up. We lunched on a mountaintop where horned toads were hiding under the lupin bushes; dove steeply down to wind along miles of canyon bottom and bring up in a detention camp on visiting day; there the road ended. This time I had read the map right, but there was nothing on it to tell me the last half of the road was closed in summer on account of fire hazard.

The following week I had to submit to some dental manipulation, so Edward took Cole and Neil on a revisit to the Wonderland of Rocks. They were back in three days, Edward with thirty new negatives including some beauties of a dead Joshua tree, its stripped arms drooping in rubbery curves. They reported that the desert was hot, the wind insupportable, and that Jack *had* fallen off the roof. Most alarming adventure: They had set up camp by the isolated rock near Jack's house, where we had camped before. As dinner preparations neared completion they were disturbed by a queer rustling sound, looked around to see an army of caterpillars pouring down the face of the rock. Many fell in the campfire at the bottom, but just as many deployed around it, to march relentlessly on in the direction of food and sleeping bags. Weston and Company broke camp in disorderly haste and surrendered the premises to the invaders.

Now it was June 12th and, Tioga Pass remaining steadfastly snowbound, we varied the desert menu by accepting an invitation to visit friends in Laguna Beach. We chose an untried southern exit from Los Angeles, wandered all morning through forests of oil derricks, and found, at the junction of US 101 and the Laguna Canyon road, a vast field of young bean plants in whose mathematical center stood three precisely spaced green trees in circular pools of shadow. That was easy. No wind, plenty of space to put the camera right where it should be, just the right light. It would have done the Petrified Forest guide's heart good to see Edward set down the camera and—bang, he had it.

In its desperate striving to look like an art colony, the town of Laguna Beach resorts to all manner of Mother Goose architecture. But business is business and people must eat. A rustic nightmare of a building, painted gourds and dimestore gadgets strewn around the entrance, an illegibly carved sign above, *Ye Olde Apothecarie Shoppe*—and, prominently displayed in a front window, a small but perfectly legible sign, Believe It or Not This Is a Drugstore.

For two days and nights we divided our time between exploring the surrounding country and returning to the unaccustomed luxury of hot baths, comfortable beds, civilized food, even a little private beach to swim from. Then as our host and hostess were anticipating other guests, we moved out to camp on the Top of the World. This was a real-estate development, that had never developed, on the crest of a high hill back of the town. The limping, unrepaired road circled around a eucalyptus grove and a couple of uninhabited houses. Off the end of a V-turn a few trees had strayed across the road; under them was just enough flat ground to hold our sleeping bags, then the ridge petered out in a rock ledge. On one side we looked down on the tiny town and beyond it over an endless expanse of Pacific; on the other, straight down to a little round valley through which ran the sandy white wash of Aliso Creek. Cattle were dark pinpoints at the base of the hills which rolled back gold and yellow and brown to the east.

Knowing the way of eucalyptus trees, I mentioned, when we settled in, that morning would likely find us dampened; but this was the only level spot and anyway a big white moon was sailing through the clear sky turning everything silver; it was too beautiful a night for practical considerations. A shout from Edward awakened me; then there was loud barking in my ear and galloping feet dying off in the distance. Two dogs in pursuit of unseen quarry had almost run over us.

We gazed around at a strange white world—or rather at the white walls of outer space, for the visible world ended quite suddenly a few feet from our sleeping bags. When the last faint barkings ceased, the silence was unbroken save for the plops of large drops of water that parted company with the eucalyptus leaves to snuggle down in our soaked beds. We dressed, pumped up the stove, and sat on the cold rocks to drink our coffee. There was no telling if it was four o'clock or eight, yesterday or tomorrow.

We were marooned on a sky island; all else had been washed away in a hush of white. We talked in lowered voices, listened to the steady drip-drop of fog from the trees, and argued about where Laguna would lie if it were still there. It was fun exploring up here. As you walked along, the mist curtains billowed out, opening a little patch of world ahead and closing one off behind. Everything looks bigger in the fog. A fence or a bush was a dark mysterious shape that loomed up threateningly until you were close enough to touch it. We found a lush tangle of yellow dodder spreading over low bushes, and a sharp-cut triangle of rock with little white wild flowers lined up before it. Somewhere beyond the fog the sun was working to warm the land. No direct light came through, but a kind of pallid indirect illumination provided Edward with all he needed to make negatives of the dodder and the rock and flowers. But everything below stayed hidden, so we packed up the damp sleeping bags and retired down the hill.

All day we commuted between the rocky coast and the world top. Edward made his first negatives of surf on the rocks, moved too close and the camera was baptized with salt spray. So when the fog finally cleared on our fourth trip up the hill, and Edward at last had just what he wanted of the pocket valley and Aliso Creek, the bellows wouldn't rack out because the sliding bed was suffering from sea bath. Edward cursed and cajoled it into behaving for four negatives, then it really quit and we had to descend to town to buy some paraffin.

We spent the night with the Ted Cooks, and the next day I said we should have a vacation. Edward said, of course, a fine idea, we deserve one. But that's the man's weakness: he doesn't know how to loaf and probably never will learn no matter how good an example I set him. First he thought he'd just get the camera out to look at a couple of potted geraniums in the patio; then there was the picket fence and the back gate, my legs in a hammock, and Ted Cook in Leica position one, i.e., lying prone, squinting up through the finder at Edward. By the end of the day the negative total was up to nineteen.

In town a letter from Ansel Adams awaited us. He had promised us a personally conducted High Sierra initiation; now he gave the word to come along any time, Tioga Pass was open at last. And in a few days the new San Simeon link of the coast highway would be open; Hanna advised us to take that route north—if we waited till fall to see it, it might be closed by slides. A week passed in setting our equipment to rights —cleaning, mending, packing, getting Heimy overhauled. While tidying up the house, which was to be turned over to Chandler for the next three months, we turned up a touching reminder. Three strange reindeer-like forms, rearing slender, branching, lavender-white antlers, reposed at the back of a dark cupboard. Old friends, forgotten companions of our maiden voyage—these were the potatoes that had been to Death Valley. Edward set a pair of them in a nest of dry leaves for one negative, in the dark cave of Heimy's luggage compartment for another.

June 29th. Farewell to the south. By now we were all expert packers, but even so it was a problem. Cole went with us as far as Carmel. His baggage, our extra clothes for the northern stay, mountains of prints for Edward's retrospective show in San

Francisco next September, darkroom equipment—trays, hangers, chemicals. On the way out of town we bought a paper to keep abreast of Los Angeles' current horror story— three Inglewood school girls missing for several days. Their bodies had been found and the police were searching for what the paper described as a Mexican-looking maniac degenerate.

Cole was driving so I sat in back busying myself with housekeeping. The tin box had not been tidied for a long time. It had begun life as a candy box shaped to represent a sea chest, and although it was far from handsome we treasured it because it exactly fitted in the center of Heimy's back shelf. It carried all manner of odds and ends that had no other logical home or that might be needed in a hurry: toothbrushes, soap box, instructions and part numbers for the gas stove, pencils and erasers, rubber bands, extra tripod screws. In it I discovered my long unused pipe and tobacco pouch. I thought I might as well light up and see how it went.

We were nearing Ventura when a motorcycle cop waved us to the roadside. All eyes quickly to the speedometer which said merely forty-two. The cop asked absently to see Cole's driving license, but fastened his eyes on me. Edward, as at all crises, swiftly produced his press card. The tension increased as the cop continued to overhaul me with a piercing eye.

Finally, "Who's that in the back seat?"

Edward, "She's a member of our party."

At the pronoun "she" the inquisitor started visibly. His gaze itemized the short hair, the faded blue shirt and pants. I knew he was wondering where the pipe had gone, or if he had only imagined it. Then, "O.K.—I'm working on this Inglewood thing. Just didn't get a good look when you went by." As we drove on I retrieved my pipe from the floor of the car, sadly cleaned it, and returned it to the tin box. Goodbye to the southland. Farewell to the desert and desert freedom. We were going into civilized lands now, where people notice.

At San Luis Obispo we turned out to the coast and presently sighted a fine field of haycocks whose irregular lines curved back to the misty black and yellow of the Santa Lucia foothills. Edward had severe wind to combat but finally made a negative.

The sign says CURVES AND GRADES FOR THE NEXT SIXTY-THREE MILES and then we begin to climb. Up and up, the road wriggles and squirms around the face of a mountain. When we get out to look over the edge, the cliff plunges straight down to an impossibly distant ocean. We were climbing back into Heimy, when a car pulled up from the other direction and the driver leaned out: "You can't g-g-go on. The r-r-road's b-b-blocked. [Pause and gasp.] I j-j-just g-g-got through. The whole m-m-mountain's m-m-m-movin'." We thanked him for the timely warning, and the frightened driver moved on at a crawl. Well, it wouldn't hurt any to go have a look, so we kept on. It was a bad slide, rocks still dribbled down onto the road, but Heimy picked his way through the debris without mishap.

There were lots of fine turnouts above the ocean, but we didn't fancy the business of camping right in the public view, so we pushed on to the Big Sur where we were welcome to use a friend's cabin whenever we were in the neighborhood. At dusk we bounced up under the oaks by the cabin; Heimy's lights swept the clearing before it, to the consternation of a doe and two fawns who had just settled on the same area for their night's camp.

Next morning an event took place to restore everyone's belief in miracles. I woke up first. It was such a unique experience, being wide awake and seeing others still asleep, that I almost laughed and spoiled everything. The clearing that held our sleeping bags ended in a sheer cliff. I walked to the edge and watched the papery foam creep over the rocks six hundred feet below. A wall of pink fog lay thick on the horizon, a pink half-moon set in the sky above it. The strong wide curves of the Santa Lucias went on to the south—ocean sucking at their feet, pink dawn clouds tumbling over their heads—until a flat-topped wedge of grey fog driven into a canyon mouth closed off the view.

Three days we sallied up and down the coast. Edward photographed kelp floating on the water, wave-washed rocks in little bays, breaking waves on a sandy beach when sunset-light turned them to molten metal. It was a good photographer's road; wide shoulders and frequent turnouts. We went so slowly, and stopped so often to look over the edge on each new turn, that Heimy seldom got off the shoulder or out of second gear. I expected the camera would get a stiff neck from pointing down over the brink so much. But instead—from that beautiful cliffside clearing we slept in— Edward developed a fine case of poison oak. While we spent a couple of days at my father's place south of Carmel, Edward's rash spread alarmingly. My father sympathized, told him he had long thought "poison oak" too mild a term for the malady, that it really should be called *vegetable syphilis*. That turned the trick. Edward was so pleased with this malignant-sounding name for his ailment that he began to improve at once.

San Francisco welcomed us with chilly fog. Brett had a flat on Greenwich Street, near the top of the Hyde Street hill. Space being restricted, we spread our sleeping bags on the front-room floor at night. First encounter with a strange darkroom brought Edward several mishaps, but he soon got used to it. What the rest of the family never got used to during sessions of heavy darkroom work was that the only entrance to the bathroom was through the darkroom.

     Warm clothes for the high mountains. Skid chains for Heimy? No. No one stocks them in summer. Shopping was easy by now. I knew the best canned brands and where to find everything—in Los Angeles. Now it was all to do over. Half my pets had never been heard of here. Meanwhile Edward made some negatives of the bay from the top of Brett's hill and more from Telegraph Hill. Then we went to Yosemite.

5 High Sierra

Lake Ediza

SAN FRANCISCO is fine because you can start any trip by going over a bridge. This time we had the Bay Bridge, immensely long and grey, and high above the chugging ferryboats. Then south and east through the yellowing hills down to the San Joaquin Valley. Perhaps we were unwise to quit the deserts after all; 97° here was more devastating than 120° there. A sign series reminded us of date milkshake days: this concerned itself with PURE ORANGE JUICE to be obtained at the GIANT ORANGE in Tracy. There was a competitor about; instructions were careful that you should find the REAL, ORIGINAL, GIANT ORANGE. After ten miles of solid advertising we came to the veritable article to find that PURE orange juice is served sweetened unless you stipulate otherwise.

Of the two routes into Yosemite Valley we chose the northern because it got into the mountains quicker. So we had the Big Oak Flat Road, sure-enough mountains, up and down them all day long, but without the hoped-for drop in temperature. Nighttime when we reached the control road—a one-way switchback down into the valley. A half-hour wait for the up-traffic to come through; then the down-traffic starts. Edward, whose first viewing it was, was properly impressed by the towering faces of pale granite that showed in the moonlight.

In Government Center on the north side of the valley, with Yosemite Falls in their backyard, Ansel and Virginia Adams have a photographic studio. There we were enthusiastically welcomed, nobly housed and fed. Plans were laid for a week's pack trip to Lake Ediza. Meanwhile we explored the floor of the valley and examined Ansel's elegant darkroom, replete with mechanical dryers, rockers, printers—Ron, Ansel's assistant, said, "You just sit down and watch them do the work." Also we speculated on what gastric adventures lay before us. Back at the start of our travels we had written Ansel to ask if he knew where we could get dehydrated vegetables. He had answered no, but anyway they were an insult to the taste buds; years of camping had taught him the needs of outdoor diet were few and simple: salt, sugar, bacon, flour, jelly beans, and whiskey.

On the eve of our departure there was a rousing party that kept its momentum well past midnight—and we were to make the six A.M. control out of the valley. Ediza was no great distance to the southeast, but to reach it we must drive north and east and south and west, more than a hundred miles in fact, before the pack-trip part of the journey began. We made the control on time, though I'm afraid none of us looked our best.

At last, the famous Tioga Road. It was worth waiting for. A narrow dusty mountain trail that wound through granite fastnesses, past emerald and sapphire lakes, under dark peaks where patches of snow still glittered. Then it plunged down a dizzy canyon—no guard rail impeding the vertical view of nethermost depths—to Mono Lake and the desert.

At Mammoth Lakes we left the pavement; at Agnew Meadow we left the car. Our belongings were stowed on three mules and we set out to do the last six miles afoot. Mosquitoes met us here, rather hungry ones, that caused us to question Ansel concerning the livestock at Ediza. Oh no. No mosquitoes there. Ten thousand feet up; too high for them.

The trail ran easily along a hillside, down to a river fording, then zigzagged steeply up two thousand feet of sheer mountainside. Edward, who for a year past had been concerned with "heart trouble," sailed up serenely. I began to waver early. More than once I would have settled down for a good nap, if it had not been for persistent mosquitoes nagging me on and for a helpful push in the back now and then from Ron. I can't do justice to the scenic beauties of the route. Dimly I saw here a waterfall, there a couple of blue lakes, now and then trees with red and yellow trunks. But all my faculties were concentrated on preserving the inertia that is supposed to make moving bodies tend to stay in motion. I had not even energy to wave away the dense clouds of mosquitoes that accompanied us as we rounded the last lake, crossed a couple of streams, climbed a last hill.

Then I sank down to enjoy the luxury of full collapse. The mules appeared, were unpacked, disappeared. The tent was set up on the edge of a stream, to see its first active service since Death Valley. Ansel had explained the mosquitoes on our arrival: these were just the few that had followed us up; when they were annihilated all would be well. We had killed ten thousand apiece now, so Ansel offered a new theory: they didn't like smoke; as soon as we got the fire started we would have peace. A big campfire was built before the tent, a smaller cooking fire near by. Oh, how those varmints hated smoke! Just had to call all their uncles and cousins to come play in it, too. Ansel made a last effort: they would go away at night when it got too cold.

Meanwhile here was dinner, hot and tasty, and an impossibly beautiful moonrise lighting dark peaks and snowbanks above us. The stream moved slowly past our camp, then went leaping down to the lake in a wild cascade that made music like wind rushing through branches. On the little hill behind us the polished rocks shone white as snow in the moonlight; beyond, on the next hill, a clearing in the trees disclosed a white ribbon of waterfall pouring evenly down dark rocks.

Next morning Ansel admitted he was beaten. There the mosquitoes were and it was most unusual. Perhaps the muggy air and all—well, maybe the afternoon shower would disperse them. The disappointment that was morning coffee should most likely be blamed on the altitude—hard to boil water and all. The beverage so called, pale tan in hue, was so rich with suspended matter that it must be strained through the teeth to avoid choking. But what of coffee at such a time? Let us prepare defenses against the enemy. Edward found a pair of gloves to protect his hands while he was focussing. He fixed a bandanna pendant from his sun helmet, stuffed the hemline under his shirt collar, tied the corners under his chin—a rather charming modified snood. I swathed my head in a large scarf, and daubed my face with lemon juice. Let me recommend that; it beats any panacea on the market. Four or five applications of lemon, blended with accumulated dust, overlays the skin with impenetrable armor that reduces the sturdiest mosquito to impotence. If you omit the ritual of face-washing, the efficacy of the preparation increases from day to day. Your comrades may object, even threaten to throw you in a lake, head first, but the protection is more than worth the price.

So let's abandon the insect question and lend an eye to the country. We were camped in a fringe of hemlocks at the edge of a terrace that overhangs the south end of Lake Ediza. The grassy smoothness of the terrace is broken here and there by heaps of polished granite and cut by a dozen meandering little streams that join in groups for the rush down hill. Volcanic Ridge, a dark forbidding mass, closes off the east; south, the Minarets—a line of jagged black spires, patched with snow that looks like cut-out bits of paper—tower in the sky; to the west Mt. Ritter and Banner Peak, both around thirteen thousand feet—story-book mountains, neatly cut triangular masses of snow and rock. Only northward the view opens out; above the lake and the wall of forest and cliff that shuts it in, we can look away over miles of curving mountaintops whose outlines grow softer and softer in the distance.

Now off to Iceberg Lake with Ron for guide and assistant camera carrier when the going gets precarious crossing slippery patches of frozen snow. Maybe it is the twenty-second of July, but up here spring is just arriving. Wild flowers bloom at the edge of the melting snow—buttercups, shooting stars, Bryanthus; the turf is soft and springy underfoot; giant grasshoppers go off like alarm clocks before our advancing

84   Tenaya Lake

86 Juniper/Tenaya Lake

94   Potato Cellar/Lake Tahoe

feet; picket pins scamper off a little distance, stand up to regard us curiously.

My heart told me we had climbed another thousand feet and I was thinking up good reasons for returning to camp, but just in the nick of time, there it was; a little lake with cakes of ice and snow floating over its inky water; across it, rising steeply from the water's edge, the Clyde Minaret, exposing a diminutive glacier on its chest. Rich hunting grounds for Edward; he worked away like mad, on icebergs, lake, minarets, tree stumps, snow and rocks. A few hours passed and I was debating: should I give up my most sensible principle and become a photographer so I, too, could retire under a focussing cloth and be safe from armies of half-starved insects? As we sat on a rock by the lake to eat our odds and ends of lunch (including jelly beans), we watched a little red bird hopping over the floating ice cakes, pecking out frozen insects—getting his lunch from the frigidaire just like city folks.

Edward set to work again, but now at each exposure he had to wait for a reluctant sun to come out of the clouds. The waits grew longer, and at last the sun went under for good. We started back to camp as the first faint rumblings of thunder came echoing up the peaks. Halfway down we encountered Ansel; we all disposed ourselves in a hollow of rocks for rest and talk. But Edward, as I say, doesn't know the meaning of the word. He instantly found a blasted triple-trunked pine with a smooth whiteness of snow beyond it that needed his attention, and when he could find nothing else to do he turned the camera on me, mosquito-rigging and all.

We returned to camp needlessly. Thunder resounded and a few drops sprinkled down—nothing you couldn't wipe up with a handkerchief—then the storm passed and the sun came out. This treatment left the air stifling, the mosquitoes ten times denser per cubic inch. Now that my heart had returned to normal, I found the main effect of the altitude was to make me acutely sleepy. I slunk into the tent, to rest my eyes for a minute as Edward would have said, and woke up two hours later. Meanwhile Edward had found more rocks and snow and wildflowers and snow-polished logs, and a beautiful clump of false hellebore growing out from under a hemlock. For the first time on any trip he used up all the holders (made twenty-four negatives) in one day.

After a rousing spaghetti dinner came the grim problem of loading. No gracious Heimy to toss a tarpaulin over; only a silly little changing bag the very sight of which filled Edward with dismay. Lying prone on the floor of the tent, he plunged into this mockery up to the elbows. The bag had been designed for something a good deal smaller than 8x10 holders; there wasn't space enough in it to shake hands with yourself and maintain any semblance of cordiality. Edward did one holder at a time, closing the film box each time so we could open the bottom of the bag, eject the empty holder and pass in a fresh one. He was muttering profanity, each moment assuring me, "Now *that* one's scratched." It took so long to get even the unloading done that Ansel volunteered for the reloading, saying he was an old hand at this and could do it in half the time. Having thus put his neck out, he got the job every night thereafter.

Next day the weather began to behave. Edward found a hill back of camp from which there was uninterrupted view to the horizon in all directions, settled down to wait for things to happen. One minute the sky was spotless blue; the next, great white laundry bags of clouds were rolling into the gaps between the peaks. Soon Edward was whirling like a dervish trying to keep up with the action on all fronts. For a time the clouds competed with the sparkling white of the snowbanks; gradually they became streaked with grey; sometimes they came so low over our heads you could almost reach up and poke your hand into the vapory eddies. At last the whole sky was blanketed and the rain came.

Our tent was a two-occupant one, so the salesman had said. By fitting ourselves in cautiously among the sleeping bags and camera cases, we proved its real capacity to be six. Besides Ansel and Ron there were two young rock-climbers in the party, and now as everyone descended from the heights wet and chilled, we stoked up the campfire and had hot toddies around. It was good to be in the warm little tent listening to the soothing noise of rain on the stretched canvas, watching the storm's progress out the open door.

An hour later we crawled out into a sparkling world; every grass blade bent under a load of silver and half a dozen new streams came noisily down the hill. The rock-climbers favored us with an exhibition, on what they called "a good practice cliff" back of camp: a smooth face of rock about seventy feet high with an overhang at the top. One of them braced himself on top of the cliff to do the belaying; the other, with the rope looped slack around his waist, edged up slowly, his hands fluttering over the rock to find finger-holds above. Edward made a negative, the tiny human being barely discernible on the vast dark face of the rock.

I thought it looked pretty easy and next day found myself a practice cliff. To be sure it was not more than fifteen feet high, but you have to begin somewhere. A six-inch ledge cut diagonally up the smooth side of a rock, and a stream rushed by below for added hazard. Ten feet above the water the ledge ended suddenly, and no amount of hand fluttering could discover a notch or a nob above me. When I started back down, feeling very foolish by now, I found the ledge had inexplicably become narrower and steeper. Then I looked down the hill and saw a party of fishermen advancing around the lake's edge. Rather a broken neck in the rapids than discovery on such a ludicrous perch! I arrived on the ground swiftly, unnerved but with full complement of limbs.

For three more days we kept to our mountain retreat. Mornings clear and sparkling; noons of gathering clouds; afternoons of thunder, lightning, and showers; evenings clear with clouds retreating over the peaks in wild sunset colors. Edward made at least twenty negatives each day: details of trees and stumps, rocks and snow; waterfalls cascading down the lightly forested slopes; pre-storm clouds and clearing clouds; Lake Ediza at sunset and at sunrise, soft light reflecting from the dark cliffs around it.

Then back to Agnew Meadow and over a couple of mountains to settle in the campground at Reds Meadow, which name we bestowed on the succulent stew that Edward devised that evening: a can of beef stew, a can of corned-beef hash, a can of tomatoes, and one of sugar peas, reduced in skillet by gentle simmering to suitable thickness.

In the morning we took the quarter-mile trail over to the Devils Post Pile. This is a basaltic formation, a half hill of standing pentagonal columns with a great heap of broken columns fallen down before it. The middle fork of the San Joaquin River runs by here, and on its bank stands a dilapidated cabin whose sagging window Ansel and Edward were both promptly at work on. On the face of a stump in front of the cabin, sundial numerals had been painted in green, along with such pertinent instructions as "Time to Work," "Time to Eat," "Time to Sleep," "Time to Play."

When the Post Pile had been dealt with we moved north to Mono Lake where the photographers grappled with the white willow skeletons that lined the shore. Tufts of bright orange grass grew at the water's edge; clouds of tiny flies rose from the wet sand and resettled as we passed; red and black fish ducks went spinning madly around on the water, getting in the way of every negative. Edward wandered down the shore to discover a delightful composition of drift twigs lying on the reeds—just a little thing nature had tossed off while whipping up the Mono waters one fine storm.

But hurry up now, let's get going! We must catch the last control into the valley: sixty miles of jouncing over Tioga bumps, skidding around Tioga turns. But not so fast that Edward failed to glimpse the fantastic mountain junipers clinging to the granite heights around Tenaya Lake. Some of them were on a cliff it looked possible to climb. It was a case of love at first sight: Edward could talk of nothing else all the way back, so we planned to return for them as soon as Ediza was developed.

We made the control by the skin of our bumpers, arrived at the Adams' Studio about ten P.M. Virginia produced a couple of cold roast chickens which we fell on without ceremony. The first bird had vanished before we began to find time between mouthfuls to relate the highlights of the trip. Swept on by the wild hilarity fatigue produces, we were all talking at once, all laughing uproariously at the feeblest suggestion of a joke.

Suddenly a white face appeared at the window, a frightened voice shrieked, "The darkroom's on fire!" Out the back door we dashed to see a red glow around the darkroom, clouds of smoke pouring out. Ansel yelled, "Negatives!," ran toward the building, Edward after him. A crowd had collected, everyone shouting advice and instructions. Everyone was asking everyone else for a flashlight. A pajama-clad figure was shinnying up the drainpipe to do something on the roof. An extinguisher appeared, a fire hose went into action, people stood looking and waiting. After a moment the red glow disappeared.

The fire was out but our work had just begun. The bathtub was filled with water; boxes, files, handfuls, of wet and partly burned negatives were dumped in. Other negatives, not yet wet, were transferred to new envelopes. Midnight came and went; the salvage crew, disposed about the bathroom and the hall beyond, worked grimly on. Not till it was all over did we recall that dinner had been interrupted and trail out to invade the icebox. Of the group, Ansel looked least like a ruined man. When we had had a well-earned drink he became positively gay, sat down at the piano and rendered an extensive Bach concert. At three in the morning we finally staggered off to bed.

So now there wasn't any darkroom to develop in. And here was a letter from Willard Van Dyke, whom we had asked to make a trip with us, saying it would have to be right away because he had to get back to New York. Our date with the junipers had to be deferred.

6 North Coast

Preview

GIVEN his choice of where we would go and what we would see in the seven days at his disposal, Willard spoke for the north coast. This is California's terra incognita. The Redwood Highway, which keeps inland for most of its length, is widely miscalled the coast road; even many native Californians don't know that a road really follows the coast north of San Francisco. Willard wanted to see all of it he could in that short time, so it was to be a swift trip—for us just a preview.

We made a late start—one in the afternoon—heading across the orange delight of the Golden Gate Bridge whose tower tops were hidden in a grey fog bank. We circled up the Mount Tamalpais Panoramic Road to no purpose—fog curtained us in on all sides. In alternate sun and fog we drove past hillside ranches with big whitewashed barns, until, near Olema, we came upon a little Portuguese graveyard. Up and down the weed-grown paths we wandered, examining the lifelike portraits that embellished the stones. Here was a child's grave, a cross of abalone shells laid over it, a broken statue at the head, the whole circumscribed by a white picket fence. This was the first time Edward had photographed a grave since his early professional days in Tropico, California, when he had had an arrangement with the local sexton to throw funeral business his way.

Tomales Bay—like Vallecitos Valley, in that Tomales comes from an Indian word meaning bay—is a long narrow inlet running back more south than east from the coast. All along its eastern shore the water is patterned with the slender picket lines of oyster beds. Here the fog rejoined us in force, rolling down over the slopes, blotting out the sun before it had a chance to set. When the road left the bay to run north between more ranches we found the picture of the day, too late. A line of chicken coops, no two of them alike, set in the center of a bare hill, with white chickens and feathers spread in a circle around them. Edward looked long and longingly but it was far too dark for such unstable subject matter.

We camped among damp dunes that night, on Salmon Creek beach. The scanty driftwood supply afforded a tiny fire around which we huddled, shivering, while the fog came weeping down like gentle rain. We inserted our sleeping bags between folds of the tarpaulin and retired to the muffled music of the surf. Next morning there were brimming lakes on the tarpaulin in the valleys between our bags, and the whole world had turned a cold wet grey. For hours we drove through a vapor-tunnel, everything blotted out except ten feet of the road ahead. Rarely there were swift glimpses down from the road to a patch of grey ocean, or up from the road to a patch of grey sheep on a grey hill.

By noon the fog had drawn back a few feet from the roadsides, bringing fences and trees into view. Edward could stand it no longer; if fog was all that offered he would photograph that. He did a fence with little white flowers behind it, a barn beyond, and slanting black tree trunks against the blank white sky. That was at Stewarts Point where a dirt road turned inland along the Wheatfield fork of the Gualala River to join the Redwood Highway. The temptation was too much; we abandoned the coast and turned our faces east in search of sun.

The road wound back through a wooded canyon where, in just a few miles, the desired commodity came filtering down upon us. We all saw the tree at once and announced it to each other with a single voice: a battered white skeleton that spread its crooked branches above a hillside of sun-bleached stubble. When we had climbed up to survey it at close range Edward became more enthusiastic over the sagging fence on the brow of the hill with dead limbs stacked against it, and—as always seems to happen for him—the proper clouds approaching rapidly.

When we came to the highway at Cloverdale it was really hot. Just shedding sweaters was not enough. I emerged from washing my face and dousing my hair to hear the gas-station man explaining to Edward and Willard that the peculiar smell of the water was associated with a dead skunk in the reservoir. We decided not to fill the canteens.

The next road back to the coast took a diagonal course that kept us all that afternoon among hills and little ranches and wandering rail fences. At dusk we came into second-growth redwood forest and passed our first abandoned lumber town— sagging buildings grouped around a silent mill. We camped on the North Fork of the Navarro at a point where it consisted mainly of a puddle ten feet in circumference and a foot and a half deep. Willard braved its perils in the early dawn and came out professing to feel like a million dollars, though from the blue looks of him I would have felt safe in knocking off several thousand.

Farther to the west the north fork broadened out to respectable dimensions, the forest thinned, and with relief we saw the fog was keeping higher than on the previous day. So here was the coast and this was Albion. Little toy houses perched on a hill overlooking a steep-walled cove. Down there at the bottom, the Albion River, green and sluggish, curving around the spit of land that held the abandoned mill. The highway looked down on it: the mill hands' empty shacks, the discarded machinery, the broken bridges, the peeling paint, the rusted metal—and over all, the heavy, silent sadness of the fog. There was no sign of life from the houses on the hill, but down in the river fish were jumping and a few trim fishing boats were tied up at the mill dock. The sun made a half-hearted attempt to strike through. Edward and Willard set up their cameras, waited a while for the light which might come but didn't, decided they liked the fog better anyway, and made some negatives.

On to the north. Through Mendocino where a really beautiful statue is placed—with no regard for photographers—atop the high cupola of the Masonic Hall. Father Time, with wings, scythe, and flowing beard, dallies with the long braids of a young lady who stands before a broken column. It was carved from a block of redwood in 1866, and every year the townspeople renew its spotless coat of white paint. The only building tops from which it might be photographed at anything like close range had steep-pitched roofs disguised by high false fronts, so we had to give up and move along.

The road itself was a delight. It would take a high turn above the water, then run back along a canyon wall until it found a place where crossing could be made on a rickety one-way bridge; then follow the other canyon wall out to seaside again and run along the narrow coastal shelf, past hayfields, weathered shacks, moss-grown fences loaded down with blackberry vines, until it turned back into the next canyon. These creek crossings came about once a mile, and every other canyon held some reminder of the boom lumber days; if it wasn't a full-fledged mill falling to pieces above its ancient log pond, then it was remains of a cable for loading ships, iron rings set in the rocks, or faintly distinguishable traces of an old building or road, now overgrown with weeds and briars.

We came in the afternoon to a place where Hanna had advised us to cut over to the Redwood Highway to avoid a stretch of the coast road that was rough and uninteresting. But Willard couldn't see it. "If we go over there, there'll be nothing but redwoods; you can't photograph redwoods so let's stick to the coast road where we might find something to photograph, and what do we care if it is a little rough?" Ten miles later we began to scrutinize the maps, but it was forty miles before we got another chance to head for the Redwood Highway; then we took it. Forty miles of an absolutely up-and-down road through impenetrable forest; no better for photography than thick fog, the only difference, we threaded a green tunnel instead of a grey one. But add to that, the road *was* rough, extremely narrow, and all the deer-hunters in the state—with trophies lashed on their fenders—were coming from the other direction. For the finishing touch Heimy had come down with grabbing brakes; touch them ever so gently and we would almost be thrown through the windshield.

So here at last the despised redwoods—impossible to photograph perhaps, but generous with their leafy, aromatic shade—their couches of piled-up needles in which your sleeping bag sinks two feet. Admittedly the camp-ground is too full of squalling babies and blaring radios, but after a while the noise abates and you lie on that softest of mattresses looking up at the giant pillars of redwood trunks that all seem to lean in over your head.

In Eureka, while Heimy was hospitalized for a brake adjustment, we wandered around examining the town. The tall wooden buildings were topped with widows' walks, water tanks were built up against the houses, the yards were neat and formal. The Carson house, a gingerbread masterpiece, sat on a hilltop, with the lumber yard that had made it possible showing over its intricate shoulders. Down by the wharf the fishing fleet was steaming in over the blue water of Humboldt Bay, and monstrous pink salmon were being tossed up onto the scales.

A warm day, so why not while away the hour with a beer? We sat at the bar, giving our attention to the details of sideboard decor. A gold plaque commemorating veterans of the Spanish American War held central place above the mirror. An ornamental plaster castle daubed with smears of bright paint reposed on the sideboard between two small wine casks that were adorned with dusty pheasant feathers. But what riveted our attention was a card, casually affixed to the edge of the mirror, covered with bold printing: SPECIAL HIGHBALL—10c—*Made with Five Kinds of Wine*—ONE OF THE BEST DRINKS. We kept careful watch, but no one ordered this reasonably priced specialty. However, when the bartender felt it was time for his pick-me-up, he poured out a half-sauterne, half-port, and sipped it approvingly; while for a customer who requested a drink in an undertone so we couldn't catch its name, he filled a highball glass one third with bourbon, the remainder with port. When the customer had tipped it down the bartender nodded his head and allowed, "Yes, it makes a good drink, but o'course y'gotta be sure t'get the purportions right."

Samoa, I can't imagine why, is the name of the narrow strip of land that locks in Humboldt Bay. There is a sawmill at one end, a lighthouse at the other, between them a waste of sodden dunes. We passed a dank night there and woke up in the thick cottony greyness that was beginning to seem a normal kind of atmosphere. I couldn't see Edward, though he was only a few feet away, but I could hear him saying, "I think this must be a wood tick and maybe you'd better look." It was, and it had made considerable progress since it had befriended him back on the north fork of the Navarro.

Performing the extraction was my last conscious act for several hours. Perhaps it was surfeit of fog, perhaps the civilized dinner we had partaken of the night before, or perhaps just watching Eurekans down their unique beverages—whatever the cause, coffee failed to revive me and I lay in the back of the car all morning hoping that every breath would be my last.

When Heimy had remained motionless for an unusual space of time, I opened my eyes reluctantly to discover myself abandoned. Heimy stood on the shoulder of a straight and empty stretch of highway; photographers were nowhere visible. Out the back window I could see a bridge and by it a sign saying, LITTLE RIVER BEACH STATE PARK. Up-river a battered barn stood among burned stumps and snags, fronted by the rotting pilings of an older bridge. I walked back to the highway bridge and looked over on the ghostliest beach I had ever seen. The sand was smooth and grey, packed hard as a pavement, cut by a shallow channel where the river moved silently across it. The sun shone wanly through the fog and eddies of mist swirled up from the water. On the sand and in the water lay enormous redwood stumps, the silvery patina of the polished wood alternating with patches of charcoal black. There were the photographers, of course, down in the midst of it; Edward photographing stumps, Willard photographing stumps, as well as photographing Edward photographing stumps. Within an hour Edward had made eleven negatives.

At Crescent City we found more redwood giants strewn over the sand. Edward used up the rest of his films and lamented the fact that there was no way to reload in daytime. But it was time for recreation anyway. The sun had come out sufficiently for the ocean to look inviting and some thoughtful picnickers had left half a watermelon reposing on yon redwood log. We swam and ate, and forever after when Edward tried to name the place he could only say Watermelon Beach.

That night we made our northern peak, camping by the Smith River only ten miles from the Oregon border. We had driven more than four hundred miles since leaving San Francisco, and the return must be made in one day less than the going. There was another morning of logs on Crescent Beach: a bleak morning, with the breakers tossing big waterlogged crabs up on the tide line, and our breakfast liberally salted with blowing sand. Edward made six more negatives and lost one when the tide crept up and sank a tripod leg during the exposure.

Near Orick there was a lookout on a cliff four hundred feet above the sea. Edward pointed the camera down at the long combers which rolled in three or four at a time with afternoon sun turning them black and gold. At Klamath Willard stopped to purchase a little meat for dinner. He hadn't been duly impressed with our stew recipes; after trying one, he had managed to work in scrambled eggs at every succeeding meal. At Moonstone Beach a sign on a store said, FREE CAMPING ON THE BEACH; we rolled down a steep dirt road to discover we were next door to Little River Beach and had a new crop of redwood monsters to examine.

We built a roaring driftwood fire in a circle of logs and Willard set to work broiling the steaks—individual ones, but each of them *family* size. Conceivably we might have disposed of that amount of meat, but the steaks proved too severe a test of our masticatory powers; so when guests dropped in unexpectedly—three homely kittens with their bashful mamma—we turned the ample remains over to them, and sat back to watch their efforts. Even they had to abandon the feast of their lives before they were in any position to kiss the cook.

The fog settled down, shrouding the campfires of several families of clam-diggers down the beach from us, turning their voices and laughter to faint hollow echoes. Edward was loading and I was lamenting that this was the night for Perseids and we wouldn't be able to see them, when Willard returned from a scouting trip to say, "Come along and I'll show you what it looks like on another planet." We picked our way by flashlight among the piled-up drift logs, down along the wet sand, until we came to a towering bifurcated rock. Between its black uprights, waves of slow-rising mist showed dimly in the light from a partial moon far out on the water. The wet sand disappeared into the vapory swirls, so we couldn't see the place where sea met sand, though we could hear the soft sucking sound of the falling tide. From a point farther north a light-house beam came swinging around like a heartbeat, lighting and leaving the mysterious landscape.

Next morning clam-diggers, strolling back and forth through the heavy greyness, told us there had only been a foot of tide that morning, but at a big tide the water came all the way up to where we had slept, and when it went out they could walk half a mile to the west to begin their digging.

South through Eureka, through the Redwoods; near Garberville the sun came out to warm and dry us. Two boys stood by a car at the roadside, flagging us; we gave one a lift into town to get a new fan belt. A college graduate from Louisiana on a vacation trip. He said they'd been to Dallas, Texas, up Pike's Peak, through Yellowstone Park, Glacier Park, Crater Lake—4,500 miles since they left home—adding that they left home a week ago. "Funny, I got a letter from my mother yesterday, and she thinks maybe we've been driving a little too fast."

Out to the coast again, to camp on a creek bank by a field of tall green oats. We heard Willard being uncommonly restless in the night, but put it down to the cumulative effect of many scrambled-egg dinners. Next morning we heard the adventure. It had begun with a roaring noise in his ear—as if an insect might be in the sleeping bag. Search revealed nothing. He lay down again; again, the roaring—redoubled in volume. He lifted the top of his sleeping bag, flashed on the light, to see a mound of earth rising where his head had been. The mole desired to surface itself there and nowhere else; Willard had diplomatically given it the right of way.

The dismal little town of Westport sits on a bluff above the grey sea. The buildings are warped and sagging, the streets are dirt ravines; if there is a population it remains invisible. Willard set off to photograph a little church; I was irresistibly drawn to the riot of blackberry vines that crowded over the fence at the edge of the highway. From nowhere appeared a woman bearing more than faint resemblance to Powerful Katrinka—the skirts billowing out, the wispy hair knotted high on the head. "Say, boy, those berries are ours."

By now I was accustomed to the fact that, to most people, short hair and pants signify boy; but I was loathe to believe that berries on the highway were other than public property. Intent on asserting my rights, I followed her into the ghost of a general store: a big room, designed to hold merchandise for every human need in a busy lumber town. The emptiness of the rows of shelves was accented here and there by little accumulations of junk: a stray ledger page, an empty bottle, a rusty pair of scissors, a dusty inkstand. All the stock was a few cans of peaches and fish stacked in haphazard formation near the door. You could hardly prattle of public domain in such surroundings; instead I asked for a candy bar. The woman went rummaging through empty drawers and boxes in vain, and I kept mentioning other brands, until at last I named a kind she had. As I paid my nickel I murmured apologies for invading her berry patch. She said that was all right, except they were all she had for canning, and if I wanted some to look up the road a way.

When I had picked a bagful from the tops of ten-foot bushes, I entered a tiny white-painted wooden church. In the vestibule I discovered a glass-doored bookcase, saw a loose-leaf binder in among the hymnbooks, and shamelessly pried. It contained the record of the Young People's Christian Endeavor Society of Westport for the year 1914. The minutes of any meeting read like this:

Sept. 5. The meeting was opened by singing song 432. After this we all said the Lord's prayer aloud. We then sang song 355. The minutes of the previous meeting were read and approved. There being no new business before the meeting it was turned over to our teacher Miss Tracy. She led us in song 57 and the meeting was closed by singing song 298.

After Westport, Fort Bragg. Here the mill still operates, so there are stores along a paved main street and people going about their business. After Fort Bragg, Noyo, with a river full of puttering little fishing boats; then Caspar with red-roofed houses and a crumbling mill. Then Mendocino and Albion. Except Fort Bragg and Noyo, they have all gone to sleep. Edward photographed the coast; breaking waves on the toothed rocks, trees and fences on the flat-topped bluffs. Another lesson in public domain: when we stopped to fill the canteens at a roadside spring a little old man came fussing up, saying the spring belonged to him, scolding lest we muddy it. And a new verb for Mr. Webster: frequent signs announced "Abaloning." Here is a north-country sign caught in passing, as nearly as print can render it:

NOtRES$PASSINgWItH

OUt PErMIt. NOS HOOTI-

Ng gOOD FISHINg.

MArK PEDOttI

Little houses on the edge of a bluff, a tiny island connected by rail bridge to the land: this was Elk, also called Greenwood. Reading from north to south: the residential section—seedy but prim; torn lace curtains at the windows, scanty gardens, broken porches. The Greenwood school—erected 1898, says the sign on its grim yellow facade. The Greenwood Inn, a low building of weathered grey wood, tiny windows boarded up, festoons of abalone shells decorating the entrance. The Elk Post Office, a new and important-looking plaster building with a whole block of main street to itself. Then a short block of business district: two gas stations, two groceries, one bar.

Well, next—groceries, milk, a place to camp. Edward set off for the milk, being advised to follow a little girl there, who was disappearing into an alley. He brought up in a backyard full of cats, chickens, and children, where an ample Italian woman dipped him out a quart from the great copper washtub. I tackled the grocery, selected a few cans, and asked about likely campsites. The grocer scratched his head. "Well, sir, go down the road here, cross the bridge, cut around sharp on that road that goes down under the bridge to the flat by the river. People that own it had the gate padlocked last year because the campers was burning up their wood and milking their cows, but I think they got it open again this year."

The last day: a hundred and sixty miles yet to be done. A day of stopping and dashing on and stopping again. There was a run-over shoe on the highway that Edward must set on a fence post to do; there were waves and rocks; there was the lighthouse at Point Arena, where the wind was so violent it threatened to sweep us into the sea. But Edward had a wind-rod by this time—a brace that runs from the front to the back of the camera above the bellows—so he worked despite the gale, while Willard and I cowered in the car with windows rolled up tight.

Finally, there was the mouth of the Russian River, at Jenner. All this had been hidden in fog when we passed northbound; now the still lagoon enclosed by a scalloped sand bar, the waves attacking the remains of an old breakwater were revealed in clear afternoon light. Edward had never had so many people in one picture: a fisherman on the rocks, two at the end of the sand bar, two people sitting on the beach. So that negative was always to be known affectionately as Edward's "Documentary."

7 High Sierra

Tenaya Lake and Mt. Whitney

A UGUST 24th we were back at Tenaya, pitching our tent in a thicket of lodge-pole pines on the edge of the lake, happy to settle down for a few days after the hectic mileage spree of the last trip. The problem of how to get up to the junipers occupied us all the first day. Edward had seen a place, he thought, where they looked easy to get to, but our first four or five attempts ended in failure. The glacial polish that gives those granite mountains their dazzling brilliance makes treacherously slippery footing, and Edward's outfit in such a place is fifty pounds of pure unmanageableness.

All day we climbed cautiously up and down the slick rocks, passing the camera and case back and forth, as one or the other of us achieved a securer vantage point. Late in the afternoon we limped into camp, exhausted from the hazardous climbing, maddened by the spectacle of beautiful junipers always above us, unreachable. A reviving swim in the lake, a hot supper, a long sleep; next morning we took up the search with renewed vigor. Almost at once we found what we were looking for: an old truck trail leading back to the base of a cliff where the climb was broken into comparatively easy stages, with at least one good juniper on every shelf.

Now life settled down into a simple routine of eating, sleeping, photographing. We got up before sunrise, rushed through coffee, drove over to the cliff. Heimy could climb up on the first slope and roll across the polished ballroom floor between the piles of glittering boulders. There I left Edward with camera, six holders, and a pocketful of dried fruit and nuts to stay him until lunch. While he climbed up to the juniper belt I drove back to camp to watch the sun rise over the lake and to feed the animals. Chipmunks came up, took bits of cracker from my hand, and went scuttering off; but if one didn't like the offering, he would hold tight to my fingers until he had sniffed over the whole hand to see if there wasn't something better. Even the birds came close for tidbits.

There was a sandy strip of beach by the camp and the water was clear as plate glass. My morning swim consisted principally of a quarter-mile walk out to where the water was waist-deep, and a frozen-footed walk back. Then I would play at being domestic, gather dead wood from the meadow for the evening fire, spread the sleeping bags on rocks in the sun. After which exertion, being 8,000 feet up, I would be so sleepy I must have a short nap. In just a few minutes the sun would be overhead which meant lunchtime. Mix up a quart of powdered milk, take a box of food and a canteen of water, sun helmets, and the other six holders, and climb up the mountain to search for Edward. By progressing from one likely looking juniper to the next I would catch up with him, usually just as he was exposing the last of the morning's films. We would return to Juniper One—a magnificent eighty-ton brute with a squat trunk supporting a mere handful of feathery green—to lunch and siesta on the hot rocks. Often the last film would be exposed before we descended to the lake for an afternoon swim which produced ravenous appetites for the evening meal. After which Edward must rush to loading before the moon got over the gap in the trees. Then we would crawl into our sleeping bags to be lulled off by the gentle lapping of the lake water.

Nights were sharply cold; days drowsily hot, except up on the mountain where a little breeze was always circulating. The few campers at the other end of the lake were screened off from us by trees and distance. Oh yes, this was the life—the life, and the place to live it. This was the desert island everyone sometime dreams of, where existence is a poem and nature all benevolence. No radios or newspapers or watches, no buildings or telephones or mosquitoes. But haven't I said photography is a stern business? And besides that, if you have a fellowship, something must be done about it. In five days Edward had photographed all the junipers in reach—some single trees accounting for eight or ten different negatives; he had photographed the granite flooring with its scattered boulders, the granite cliffs hemming in the lake, the lake itself, the cliffs alone, reflections of pines in the water, roots in a stagnant pool—everything he could find in a radius of several miles. Then, too, Ansel had said he must go down the east side of the Sierra to make a negative of Mt. Whitney for a book, and why didn't we join him? So really it was time to go.

All the last day we pretended we were going to leave in a few hours, but knew we weren't, because Edward could always find one more thing to photograph, or remember a juniper he hadn't seen in a certain light. That night a brace of bears came snuffling around the tent; Edward roared at them, they growled back. I went to sleep then, but Edward stayed awake most of the night engaging in duets with his animal friends. Next morning he was really ready to leave.

As soon as Edward had developed his Tenaya loot in the rebuilt Adams darkroom, we went dashing off to Mt. Whitney with Ansel. On this trip we really saw the Sierra for the first time. To be sure you can see some snowy peaks from the west side when the visibility is good, but there are miles of foothills and medium-sized mountains leading gradually up to them. The east side of the range rises abruptly from the Owens Valley, a towering perpendicular wall of granite, an endless battlement of ragged peaks biting into the sky.

It is time to rename the Owens Valley the Los Angeles Desert, since that city has aqueducted all the water out, leaving deserted farms edged by lines of skeletal poplars, fields and pastures disappearing before the advancing sagebrush. As we drove south down the dry valley, Ansel kept pointing out Mt. Whitney and changing his mind; hardly a peak in the Sierra but had held the title briefly when at last we came to Lone Pine where we could have looked up at the big chief, except it was then too dark. So although we drove up to Hunters Flat to make camp on Mt. Whitney's front porch as it were, we didn't see the peak until next morning, when, ambling around with our mugs of coffee, we looked up through a gap in the trees to the high white granite spire shining in the sunrise.

During the next three days we drove up and down from mountain to desert almost constantly. Between Lone Pine and the Sierra wall lies a line of low brown humps, the Alabama Hills. Remains of an ancient mountain range, their substance was the now familiar desert granite; but the wind-polished surfaces we were accustomed to were here replaced by rough flaky surfaces that looked like peeling wallpaper. And, too, the boulders were grouped on isolated hills; so it was quite different from the Mojave formations we had seen. That first morning, while we were down in the Alabama Hills, a storm swept up from nowhere to settle over the Sierra. In panic I remembered our sleeping bags, spread out to air on Hunters Flat; but Edward and Ansel were having too much fun photographing the downpour that half obscured the peaks to worry about so trivial a matter. Luck was with us; the rain held off from the camp until the moment of our returning. We covered food and bedding with the tarpaulin and crouched under the semi-protection of a pine to eat our lunch.

Descending from Hunters Flat, the road comes out of a wooded canyon to zigzag down the bare face of the mountain. We arrived on the uppermost zig that afternoon to find celestial activity at its height. The whole southern end of the Owens Valley was visible from here—from tiny pin points that were junipers at the bottom of the grade, over the pale broken land of the sage desert, to the Inyo Range in the east. Brilliant patterns of cloud shadows spread over the valley, the Alabama Hills, the white alkali blot of Owens Lake to the south—and over all stood a perfect arch of rainbow.

Stop the car! Out with the cameras! for a race between the photographers and the elements. Every second the light is shifting as the cloud-shadow patterns go racing by down in the valley. At one moment the Alabama Hills are a sooty menace of silhouette; at the next they are dazzling in a downpour of blinding light. Ansel and Edward work feverishly, stopping down, setting shutters, pulling slides, making negatives in split seconds. Rain sweeps over our mountain perch. Between negatives the photographers wring out their focussing cloths like wet towels.

Then the crisis passes. The clouds roll back to form a single grey band against the Inyos. We dry off the cameras, roll on down to the valley, in that strange storm light that turns all the roadside pebbles yellow and violet and endows the most commonplace objects with supernatural radiance. As we look out over the desert valley a tiny silver airplane comes dropping out of the cloud bank, flashes and dips, curves up against the blue sky, dives into the grey cloud mass once more.

The following afternoon we found an abandoned soda works on the edge of Owens (mostly dry) Lake. There were tumbled-down kilns, rusty boilers, a fascinating assortment of wrecked machinery—but in addition there was a relentless wind blowing powdery white dust that soon left you gasping and choking. Edward made several negatives—in one, of a wrecked car, he used part of the camera's shadow to complete his composition. And here we discovered the shoes to end all shoes: they had been fancy footwear in their day—high button shoes, the button strip was still red, the rest had been transformed by desert exposure to a brilliant coppery green. We took them back to the Alabama Hills where Edward looked for the proper rock ledge on which to photograph them, while I explored some of the side roads that wound among the rocky hills. In a dry wash, between the tumbled boulders and the naked sagebrush, crouched a cluster of shacks, warped by sun, battered by wind. Only the sign in front had proud fresh paint on it, Cozy Glen.

North in the Los Angeles Desert, nee Owens Valley, through forests of skeleton trees. Dead white or burned black, the tree trunks stand beside the shiny new power standards; the shiny parallels of the power wires cut through the delicate lacing of dead twigs and branches like the lines of a musical score. And over all this fantastic forest of death and civilization, towers the grim east wall of the Sierra. We followed roads back and forth across the northern end of the valley, and Edward and Ansel had a busy day of it. Then, late in the afternoon, the customary cross-mountain dash to make the last control into Yosemite Valley.

On our way back to base we took the Big Oak Flat route. What with the perishing heat, and what with an hour's roadside labor to remove the embedded remains of a broken tripod screw, we reached Buck Meadow Lodge feeling the need of refreshment. A dark interior with a few tables and a long bar; a mechanical record-player giving off IN THE GOOD OLD SUMMERTIME; a sad-looking little bartender, tied into a big white apron, his remaining grey hairs combed carefully up over his bald pate. I throw the place into panic by asking for a milkshake.

While the bartender reels from the request, an efficient-looking woman in tailored suit and white frilled blouse steps forward, says, "Certainly," and pulls up her sleeves. No chocolate syrup; how about vanilla? Or strawberry? Fine. Strawberry will be fine. Out with a jug, pour, halt. Out with another jug and pour some more. A size-up look at me to see if I will be able to take it. "May taste a little funny," she remarks, searching for the plug for the mixer. "I got some vanilla in before I saw it wasn't strawberry." Plugged in, the machine commences to gurgle in a terrible soprano. "Got it too full," she shouts in explanation to the little knot of curious onlookers who have gathered to witness the unique performance. "It'll slop over in a minute."

The beverage is poured dramatically into a beer glass; tailored-suit steps back to survey her handiwork proudly. The first sip is a shock to my palate but I manage to nod my head approvingly, whereupon the audience breaks up, breathing sighs of satisfaction and relief.

8 One-Week Trip
False Mother Lode

IT WAS September 14th, and we wanted to be in town on the 22nd for the opening of Edward's retrospective show at the San Francisco Museum. Where should we go for a week? We decided to take a look at the Mother Lode country; and since Edward was not likely to find much there, we felt we might as well relook at a few coast spots on the way.

Wednesday, September 15th. Late afternoon. We were in the town of Point Reyes at the head of Tomales Bay, trying to get on the road that follows the west shore. By missing a turn-off we arrived among backyards and barns to see a fresh-painted green pullman car set down in the middle of a field. The sign on it said, POINT REYES BRANCH MARIN COUNTY FREE LIBRARY.

The west-shore road quits the bay to wander overland through grey fog and low hills plastered with wind-stunted brush. Everything is fenced and private. No chance to camp. We were about to turn back when out of the fog appeared a black and white sign on a gate:

WELCOME TO DRAKES BAY
Sheltered Beach for Bathing and Picnicking
25c per car   Pay at Farmhouse

Across the bare pasture into the farmyard: whitewashed barns, dark cypresses, a straggling flower garden with chickens pecking in it. A small boy came running out:

"You wanta go to the beach?"

"Can we camp there?"

"Mmmm. I guess so."

"All right then." Three dimes changed hands.

"Uhhhh. Haven't yuh gotta quarter?"

"No. Keep the other nickel yourself."

Executing a pagan dance of triumph, the boy galloped on to open the gate for us.

Steeply down to a reedy marsh; a boarded-up grey shack in a cypress clump at one end, a driftwood-cluttered beach at the other. The wind blew down from the hills, strong and cold. We sat by a crackling driftwood fire to eat Swedish fishballs in brown sauce, maple sugar for dessert. When we got into our sleeping bags the wind went down and mosquitoes arrived. Late in the night we woke up to hear a boat chugging; we looked out at the bay to see it all alight with little fishing boats moving out on the tide.

Thursday, September 16th. I climbed up from the depths of sleep to hear Edward saying, "Get up. We have lots of animals." Opening one eye and then the other, I saw a few birds, then three lumbering brown horses that ambled down to the surf and frolicked off along the foggy beach. We sat on a log to drink our coffee while seagulls walked about on the wet sand looking gloomy.

Back to Tomales Bay for negatives of mud flats. Around the bay and over the hills: Look at that! One fence, three cows, two houses. Edward set his camera up. He willed the cows to walk where he wanted them; they did. He willed them to "hold it" for a one-second exposure; but one of them flicked at a fly.

Here was the line of chicken coops again, but the light was all wrong and the chickens were all wrong. Next, the Bodega coast—a strip of rocky shore and State Park beaches between Salmon Creek and the Russian River. Edward had seen possibilities at Duncans Point, on the return with Willard. Then, it was too late to work. This time the fog had settled low and thick. I went to the gas station on the point, "What time is it and do you think the fog will lift?"

"Three o'clock, and not likely today."

Several hours of driving time were left. We thought we might as well make a start toward the Mother Lode.

East through the hills, the ranches, the fenced lands; Freestone, Sebastopol, Santa Rosa. South to Sonoma and east again: spreading oaks on smooth rolling hills, hillside orchards, eucalyptus windbreaks, fences and fences. For a quarter, a gas stationer let us camp in his back yard, not bothering to give notice that mosquitoes were there ahead of us.

Friday, September 17th. The cool mist we woke up in soon lifted and the sun came out hot. All morning we wandered on side roads among the pale yellow hills, cornfields, pear and prune orchards. Sleek horses and cows watched us from the pastures; a buzzard sat on a fence post, waiting for Heimy to pass so he could get back to the slain rabbit on the highway. Approaching Fairfield, we were watching a line of bare hills to the north. The sculptured yellow mass beckoned irresistibly and we turned off the highway.

In this country side roads never go straight to anything: you approach your objective obliquely, by a series of right-angle turns around the corners of the farmers' fields. Five miles of this procedure brought us to our objective—but in that five miles we had taken up so much of the land's gradual rise that instead of big, shapely hills, we found only smooth little knolls. But if we didn't find what we came for, then there was always something else. The dry grass that clothes these little knolls was bleached to a dazzling silvery-white; before the knolls were black poles and wires and a bit of black oiled road—all of which delighted Edward to the extent of three negatives.

What a day! We pulled at the canteen and complained of the heat as though we had never served a desert apprenticeship. We crossed the Sacramento River and passed through the State capital in weather that only Hanna would describe as *warmish*. The valley was flat and dull and dusty. Soon we would be at the side road that turns off to the Mother Lode.

"Asleep, Edward?"

"Hnh? No. Just resting my eyes."

"Going to be hot up there."

"Mother Lode? Yes. Guess it will be."

"Don't think you'll find much to do."

"No. Suppose not."

"More literary interest than photographic."

"Want to see it sometime, won't we?"

"Sure. Sometime. Awfully hot now though."

"Anything else around that's cooler?"

"Well—there's Tahoe, of course—"

"All right. Why not?"

We passed the turn-off and settled back, immensely pleased with ourselves for having changed our minds so easily. Up into the brown and yellow foothills we climbed. Oaks were replaced by feathery pines; the roadbanks were half-moons of red clay. Up the main street of Placerville, a long line of tight-wedged, false-fronted buildings; out of the town and into the forest.

Cooler now, as we climbed in dusk past the elevation markers: two thousand, three thousand. Off the highway, steep down the bank, to the Maple Grove Public Camp on the south fork of the American River.

Maple Grove Stew: 1 can solid-pack tomatoes; 1 can whole kernel corn; 1 can condensed ox tail soup. Dinner by bright moonlight, and then perhaps, we thought, a bath. *Perhaps,* because the south fork hasn't made much provision for that sort of thing. However, there was one pool four feet long and two feet deep that would accommodate us one at a time, and the water was still warm from the day's sun.

Saturday, September 18th. For the second (and last) time in Guggenheim history, I woke up and got up first. Nothing else notable happened until some miles along the road we came to our first regulation highway sign saying, SLOW—DEER CROSSING. The walls of the river canyon were lined with summer homes: wood or stucco cottages, rusticarved signs displaying their names. That day we kept tally on the favorites: 14 JOURNEY'S ENDS, 11 BIDE A WEES, 23 WHISPERING PINES.

Down the grade and into Meyers, which was once a stop for the pony express. At the end of the line of tall pine buildings was a little potato cellar, its snow-polished board front crisscrossed with rust tracks from the nails. I slowed down and we looked.

PHOTOGRAPHER: "Pretty nice."

CHAUFFEUR: "I should say so. Want to stop?"

PHOTOGRAPHER: "N-no. I guess not."

One mile later—

PHOTOGRAPHER: "I don't know . . . . Maybe I should have taken a look . . . ."

CHAUFFEUR: "Shall I turn back?"

PHOTOGRAPHER: "No-o-o-o. I guess the light wasn't very good."

Two miles later—

PHOTOGRAPHER: "I'm sorry; think we better go back, after all."

CHAUFFEUR: "! XxxX XxxX XxxX !"

Mostly the lake was blocked from view by private property along the shore. In one or two places you could look down on it and Edward made a few negatives at Emerald Bay and in the State Park on Bliss-Rubicon Point. Finding (on the map) a Rubicon River in the vicinity, I watched the signs at each creek-crossing—hoping to be able to enter casually in the log, "At noon we crossed the Rubicon, near its headwaters . . . ." Disappointed in this matter, I fell back on a forgotten nugget of California scandal. Once a governor's name was bestowed on this noble body of water. "Tahoe" has come in with usage, but the legally correct name is still "Lake Bigler"—which form of address I proposed to use freely, until I had crossed the Rubicon.

Sunday, September 19th. There were no people there. Stores were boarded up. There was sharp cold in the air and the first snow was expected any day. We took US 40 north to Donner Lake, and up to Donner Summit where a steam shovel awaited our coming in sabbath idleness. Edward had fun with the clamped jaws of the scoop in front of the distant lake. In long waits between negatives, when the sun retired in heavy clouds, we watched the stream of Sunday travelers that rolled up, paused to snap, and rolled on.

Out from the ranks of the kodakers stepped a young man who announced that he has some pretty good pictures in the car—maybe we would like to see them? Edward said sure, bring them out. They were good enough snaps; Edward said, yes, they were fine; the lad admitted he thought so, too. Then said the unfailing, "I bet that camera of yours takes pretty good pictures." Edward said he guessed it was like any other camera, it depended on what you did with it. The young man was struck all of a heap by this revolutionary idea; he laughed with false heartiness—as one pretending to enjoy a joke while knowing he'd missed the point—and backed hastily away.

Over the summit and down to Lake Van Norden—an artificial (Power Company) lake to hold water from melting snows. It was three-quarters dried up, exposing a wide strip of mud flat dotted with water-worn stumps. Inch-high grass had sprouted between the stumps, and everywhere—in the mud cracks, on the stones, around the stumps—there were hordes of tiny brown frogs. They flew out in clouds from our feet as we walked over the boggy ground. Edward found everything to suit him: the stumps, the lake, the light, the clouds—even a bird who came to sit on a stump in the foreground of one negative.

The Cold Springs Public Camp was a few miles down the road. With a whole meadow full of rotten wood and a river bank of stones to draw on, we built a big fireplace and a monstrous fire. For the first time in two days we were warm enough to peel down to our primary shirts. We wrapped the sleeping bags in extra blankets and tarpaulin, turned in under a clear moon-bright sky. Off in the woods owls hooted and screeched; up at the summit a long freight roared and clattered through the endless snowsheds.

Monday, September 20th. In spite of the elaborate heat-holding system, it was a night of cold feet. A big coffee fire to thaw us out. The grapes were so nearly frozen through, they clicked against our teeth. Back to Van Norden for another bout of stumps. Perhaps it was the cold slowing up our faculties: Edward—and it was the first time since 1920, he said—broke his ground glass. There was a spare in the car, so all was well.

Down the cold mountains, into the warm foothills, into the hot valley. Emigrant Gap, Dutch Flat, Grass Valley, Rough and Ready. Perhaps the old gold towns are picturesque, but the countryside, laid waste by hydraulic mining, is horrible: mountainsides are scarred and gouged, washed away to the naked earth; ravines are choked with debris piles. And now, along the gravelly river beds, the latest crop of gold seekers is camped, hopefully panning; little lines of Monday wash flap in the sun beside the old model cars.

One of Edward's uncles came out in the gold rush, died of fever, was buried in Marysville. Another uncle, now ninety-four, asked us to look for his brother's grave. We got directions to the town's oldest graveyard, found to our dismay it covered several blocks, parked in the center and started working out. Edward found the stone among the first half dozen he looked at:

RUFUS F. BRETT
Died May 5, 1852
aged 20 yrs 10 mos
God gave, he took
Be well resigned
He doeth
All things well

Edward made a negative of it for his uncle. We wandered a while among the old stones, then moved on west across the flat hot valley.

Down the straight road we drove, with fiery sun in our eyes, the flat fields spreading out before, beside, behind us. The level land is broken only in the north by the noble pile of the Sutter Buttes—remains of an old volcano. At last the sun dropped down behind the coast range and a little stirring of breeze came to cool us. When the road right-angled around the corner of a plowed field, we looked back on a sight of miraculous beauty: beside the dark profile of the buttes a full, orange-tinted moon had come up in a sky that was blue at the hem and lavender above.

We asked in Colusa, but no one had ever heard of a place to camp. We asked again in Williams. Why yes, about twenty-four miles along there was a service station that had free camping. Columbus was surely wrong; the world was flat and would always be flat no matter how far we drove. Oh, for a Forest Service camp! A Maple Grove, or a Cold Springs: tables and faucets and fireplaces and out-of-season solitude.

What was the matter with Heimy? He was losing power. Beyond belief, of course, but we had actually come to the end of the flat land; the road was tilted up into the hills. "Look!" said Edward, but I was already looking: round black pools on the bare white slopes, in endless variety of form and pattern. Even by moonlight we could tell that these were the hills and oaks Edward had been looking for ever since we came north.

We followed an enchanted road through the silent black and white landscape. A good two-laned pavement without a store or a gas station or a house beside it; sometimes not even fences to the fields; and never a car to meet or pass us. We had done the twenty-four miles twice over when a little light showed on the highway ahead. The free camp was a flat bit of stubble field between the gas station-store, the house, and the windmill. After a few bites of cold supper we fell instantly asleep, in spite of the moonlight that was bright as day and a fearful racket from the generator.

Tuesday, September 21st. The night before, determined to buy something in exchange for the free camp, we had asked the proprietress if she had (one by one) dinner, sandwiches, coffee, fresh or canned fruit. She said no to each, explaining it was out of season. This morning we renewed the attack, discovered the only thing she had was beer. A little early in the morning to begin on that, but after we had retraced last night's route for negatives of hills and oaks, we returned to refresh ourselves and to even the score.

A blasting hot day. We were close to the southern elongation of Clear Lake; what was wrong with stopping for a swim? The first road we tried landed us in a mining wasteland where signs posted every few feet said, DANGER! HEAVY BLASTING GOING ON. The second brought us to Clear Lake Park, where we staggered out over sharp rocks into grey-green pollen-filled water. A hot buzzy sticky day; you could have baked bread inside Heimy with all the windows open. South through the sunburned hills to Calistoga; west through the heat-charged hills to US 101; down the Russian River to the sea.

In a little town on the river road, we were the last customers for dinner. The moment we were out of the door the Redwood Grill closed up for the night—at seven o'clock. So here we were at the coast again. We had crossed the state twice in the last five days; we had experienced a swift succession of varied climates; but the fog we left on Duncans Point had stood faithfully by to greet us on our return.

Wednesday, September 22nd. Anywhere but California, what was coming down would be called rain. We shivered in the descending mist and warmed our hands on our coffee cups. A big black and white dog came to see us—white sox, white bib, a waving white banner of tail. We named him Rover and took him for a walk along the beach. Through the weeping fog a laughing party of women and children came flocking onto the wet sand. Adults were attired in skimpy summer beach-wear; children stripped off their scanty garments and tumbled into the water. Even Rover looked astonished at their obvious enthusiasm.

When we drove up onto the point the fog had lifted to make a little of the coastline visible. At one corner of the headland stood a grey weathered sign:

WARNING
STAY ON THE BEACHES

14 PERSONS have been swept away from rocks
and ledges around this headland. NO BODIES were
ever recovered.

Unexpected groundswells coming at long intervals
SWEEP THE ROCKS.

Anyone within 25 feet of ocean level is in danger
all the time.

HEED THIS WARNING

We had seen the big sign on the highway in front of this point: SEE DEATH ROCK. Now we decided that name must apply to the detached bit of cliff right below the warning sign—the rock that was even now appearing in the foreground of a negative of the long grey beach and coastline.

I walked over to the gas station, returned Rover to his master, and asked about the sign. Oh Lord no; no fourteen people had ever drowned here, but maybe four or five had. So this was the answer to why Death Rock: A man high up in the Native Sons was swept off the rock and drowned. The Native Sons thereupon came with a load of dynamite to blow the rock into the sea. All morning they drilled holes; in the afternoon they set off the mighty charge; the smoke cleared and a few pebbles dribbled down into the sea. As a less costly alternative to bringing another load of dynamite, they erected the warning sign, named the lump Death Rock. The narrative ended in a reminiscent chuckle: "Yes, it was the Native Sons named the thing 'Death Rock'; us oldtimers always just called it 'the hog-back.' "

On to Tomales Bay for oyster beds in a luminous fog sunset and a lone white horse on a grey hill. We stopped to eat in a little restaurant in Fairfax, where there was a constant rushing in and out of people who came to speak to the proprietor in hurried whispers. We asked what was going on. "Well, you see all the working people in town have organized into one big union. Tonight they have a picket on a bar down the street. First time anything like that ever happened in this town; people don't know what to make of it."

Fairfax, too, rolls up the sidewalks early. We drove down the quiet store-dark street. At the end of the block we saw the picket—a red ribbon spread across his chest— pacing slowly back and forth in the lonely light from the open door of a corner saloon.

On through the dark countryside, the sleeping towns. When we came out of the hills above Sausalito, a strange moon with a corner bitten off was riding up through racing black clouds. Below us lay the orange bridge with all its gay lights; a puddle of moonlight lay on the yacht harbor; a deep cloud shadow covered Alcatraz, and through it moved the line of tiny lights from the windows of a ferryboat.

9 Northern Circuit

Rain in the North

REALLY it was foolish to be starting on another northern trip this late—especially the longest one of all, a circuit of the whole top end of the state. But there was so much yet to see; and suppose we did run into a little weather—hadn't we warm clothes, skid chains, plenty of food to withstand even siege by snow? Well, as I say, it was foolish; but here we were, late in the afternoon of September 28th, northeast of Sacramento on State Highway 49, congratulating ourselves on having found a perfect campsite in the midst of the farmlands.

Neither fence nor sign barred our way to the clump of live oaks on the grassy knoll. But when we had turned in early under bright stars, we ceased to congratulate: the night came alive with a hideous roaring as two engines—puffing backwards—pushed a long line of freight cars up the grade a hundred yards from our heads. The performance was repeated at intervals all through the night and we got little enough sleep between trains.

Next morning we started north through the wooded foothills, our course punctuated by sleepy little gold towns. We were pulling out of North San Juan when a tall man in patched brown clothes and needing a shave signalled us from the roadside. Could we give him a lift as far as Camptonville? No room in back, but he could ride in front with us. He thanked us profusely. Said we were saving him a long walk and he had walked twenty-three miles yesterday. Said he was going up to one of his mines; he had two of them over there—and he gestured vaguely out the car window. Said he'd been down here looking for his dog, a little screw-tail bull pup: "I tracked him down this far but didn't find him. Me and the dog, we live all alone in a cabin up here at my mine. . . . Yes, I been in the mines twenty-five years now, and that's the funny part because I'm really a cartoonist. . . . "

The monologue, reinforced by occasional prompting, meandered on in alcoholic haze. There was the story of Fitzsimmons hitting him between the shoulders, of Jeffries watching him fight, of how he was cartooning when Bud Fisher was an office boy, of how he had just leased one of his mines to three college boys and he had three thousand dollars waiting for him down in San Francisco—all he had to do was go down there and get it.

When we passed houses or cars he drew his hat low on his forehead and looked the other way. Every yarn was punctuated with, "Of course these things may sound strange to you, but every word is gospel truth—I never lie"; also frequent references to his need for some beer. At last it came out that he had a bottle in his pocket, but none to offer us. We overrode his courteous protestations. Having disposed of his draught, he decided not to stop at Camptonville, and became even more talkative and less lucid. For example, there was the story of the two big bosses.

They were big shots—he knew they were big shots because he had seen them in a big office building in San Francisco—and they drove up one day, and he was sitting in front of his cabin, and they came over, and he got on all right—had his spectacles on and held his handkerchief in his hand, being nervous—and everything went fine, and he was all right, and they said can you cook for ten men, and he thought they were joking and said sure, he used to cook for twenty-five, and they said well, the boys will be along tonight and you'd better have some food for them, and he still thought they were joking, and then they made him take them all over the hills, showing them places and pointing things out, walking around in the hot sun, and he was feeling plenty sick but he held out all right, and then they left and said the boys would be along that night, and he thought it was a joke and went on home and went to bed. Then there was an awful racket, and sixteen fellows he'd never set eyes on arrived with a lot of grub, so they introduced themselves to him, so he cooked the grub, and in the morning he had to make seventy-five hotcakes for them, and he had to every morning for a week, and then they all left, but first they came and told him he was a better chef than the one at the Palace Hotel.

By this time he was calling Edward "Frank" and me "Ma'm." He said, "You know it's not good living by yourself all the time and never seeing people. That's what I need, to get to talk to people sometimes. I don't want you folks to think I'm a *conformed* drunkard, because I still think there's hope, and we might all meet again sometime. You know, Frank, what I'm going to do when I get that money? I'm going to get out of here and go to Hollywood. You see, I sing; and I know a man that told me I'm the greatest singer in California, and I'm going down there to Hollywood and get me a partner to join up with me. . . . "

Edward asked what kind of songs he liked to sing. "Oh, I'm an oldtime singer;

none of this new-fangled stuff. I wouldn't have it. I wouldn't have a radio up in my place—all that stuff all the time. Now you know Caruso. I heard Caruso and Lillian Nordica and—and all those people when they came out here and sang, and Lord! It was enough to raise you right up out of your boots. Well, *that's* the kind of singing I do."

He asked us to let him out by a little roadside drink emporium. Edward cut short an elaborate dunning speech, handed him the fifteen cents for another beer. From his stance on road and running board he announced in parting, "I'm fifty-six, been married three times; but if I have a woman around I always cut out the liquor—you can't drink with a woman, you know—and then when I quit drinking pretty soon there'd be a row. . . . Well, you folks have been mighty nice to me. . . . If you're ever in trouble, remember my place—plenty of grub—no questions asked. . . . "

Downieville, Sierra City; mine towns in steep-walled canyons. Over Yuba Pass, down to Sierra Valley. We rub our eyes, look, and look again. Big, powerful workhorses moving around in the yellow pasture, and without any doubt or trick of the light, their color is blue! Not sky blue, of course, but bluer than navy blue. Most common view of agrarian life: ramshackle barn, house needing paint and repairs, rundown yard, with a shiny new-model car in it. The country is dry and hot, the road indifferent to bad. We look forward to a swim in Honey Lake, are amazed and outraged to find it a dry lake.

Having recrossed the Sierra, we entered Lassen Park early next morning, and left it the same afternoon. In the few hours we were there Edward photographed Lassen with a steamy cloud on its head, made five negatives in the "Devastated Area." The latter is the product of the 1915 eruptions, which denuded a wide sector of all vegetation. Several friends had described it to Edward as a chaotic ruin—forests of dead trees, upturned roots, fallen trunks. Not being photographers they had failed to mention that most of this ruin is now mixed with growing aspens, small trees, and bushes. Pictorially, it is no longer a devastation, but rather a splendid picture of nature's progress in reforestation.

Making the negative of Lassen—first one of the trip—Edward discovered that both of his shutters (fresh from overhaul at the camera hospital) were out of order; the set speeds so far off that, on a 1/75th sec. exposure, one stayed open three seconds. We were four hundred miles from base; nothing for it but to rely on bulb exposures throughout the trip. Most thought-provoking sign in the park was at Lake Helen, stating it was named for "The first white lady to climb Lassen Peak."

From the feel of the air, it would surely snow that night so we decided to keep on our northeastern course which should take us out of the mountains by nightfall.

As we climbed the long easy grade up the Bieber Mountains late that afternoon, our hurry was repaid. Below us lay the flat fields of the Fall River Canyon, already indistinct in the dusk; beyond them a broken terrain of hills, ridges, and cinder cones, leading back to the distant peaks of Lassen and Mt. Burney; above all this, great zeppelin clouds sailed through delicate curtains of cirrus in the flaming sunset sky. Edward made the bulk of his Lassen negatives from a distance and was well pleased with the take.

The girl at the Gas & Eat station in the valley said "lots of them" camped back there at the foot of the hills, down the road past the cemetery. So there we went to settle in a pine wood. Instinct told us to put up the tent, but the sky was clear and we were lazy, so we folded the tarpaulin up over our sleeping bags and were just comfortably installed when the first drops fell. I roasted all night in my sleeping bag; Edward retreated to the car and froze.

Coffee by a fire in the gentle rain, in a wet and dripping world. All day we explored the northeast corner of the state, and all day the downpour continued. We drove through alternate strips of forest and farmland; haystacks in the fields with individual rail fences around them so the cattle couldn't nibble. Little towns, old houses, wooden churches, windmills. Dwellings and farmsteads scattered thinly over the miles of juniper forest and sage land, rocky river canyons, dry lake valleys at the foot of dun-colored mountains.

When we asked in Alturas about the road into the Lava Beds National Monument, we were told "Dirt, but good." And would it likely be raining there? "Oh, yes! That's a storm center!" In a slough of black mud, between lines of potato cellars, we proceeded sometimes forward and often sideways to Tule Lake. A night of rain, a day of rain, of cramped, wet discomfort. Only the voluptuous vision of hot showers and dry beds sustained us through the last skidding miles.

"Autocamp? No. Afraid not. Town's full of potato pickers. Not even tent-space left." Eighteen more muddy miles to the camp in the Lava Beds, and it was already dark. Well, at least we could get some dinner here. The small hot room was already crowded with potato pickers. We found a table, ordered the regular dinner:

CLAM CHOWDER
(1 cup hot, diluted, canned milk, containing salt,
pepper, and waistband of 1 clam)
SALAD
(1 thin cross section lettuce, supporting 1 thinner

cross section hardboiled egg, supporting mayonnaise size of a pine nut)

ROAST VEAL

(1 generous heap of glutinous matter, two thin slices of possibly veal laid tenderly over it, the whole baptized with water brown fluid)

accompanied by:

canned peas   potatoes
(half-heated)   *(disguised as cole slaw)*

DESSERT

(2 cubic inches pink jello draped with 1 thimbleful whipped cream)

followed by:

1 cup brown fluid (to be distinguished from what covered the main dish only by its greater transparency)

We left the eating house in silence, for what was there to say? Heimy stumbled on through the wet night, swimming hub-deep puddles, slithering through mud without end. For the fact that we did finally reach the campground, all credit to the road-wise Heimy; I admit I had little to do with it. I do remember the struggle to set up the tent in the rain, the clamminess of a damp sleeping bag, then what the writer-folk call merciful oblivion.

When we had made coffee in the tent next morning, the weather granted a truce, during which we walked to a hillock near camp that promised a view. Small scattered junipers provide the only green in this landscape; all else is sharp black branches of dead trees, white branches of dead bushes, black openings of caves. Between the dark lava trenches, spongy grey soil supports tufts of pallid grass which exactly duplicate the appearance of the bleached blond who has carelessly let her hair grow in black at the roots.

A strange and savage landscape it is, in the alternating sun and shadow of the clearing sky; the rough lava shining wetly, the bare branches and pale grasses motionless, dripping. This is a part of what the pioneers called *The Dark and Bloody Ground of the Pacific*. Here California's last and bloodiest Indian war was fought, when a small band of Modocs entrenched themselves in the lava caves that honeycomb the region, and for several months held off a far superior white force. It is a land of violent contrast:

132　Surf at Orick

the surface growth is blasted by drought, but down in the caves there are rivers of ice, frozen waterfalls, ferns and moss kept green all year by moisture from steam-vents.

We set out to explore the loop road around the Monument.

EDWARD: "I thought you were to turn north?"

CHAUFFEUR: "I did."

EDWARD: "Don't be silly. You're going south."

CHAUFFEUR (*unblessed with any sense of direction*): "This is the way we came in, and the map says we came in from the north."

EDWARD (*with tempered scorn*): "I suppose you think the sun rises in the west up here!" Such cold logic forced me to reverse my direction, but, still unconvinced, I pulled up at Headquarters, asked the ranger. My direction was right; so was the sun's position, since it was on its way to setting in the old conventional place. All at once we realized what a thoroughly good sleep we had had.

Four days we spent in the Lava Beds—four days of rain and cold; of struggling to light a fire of wet wood in the grey dawn; of pouring hot water over Heimy's doors because they were frosted shut; of driving all day in rain, or with rain all around us. Edward photographed landscapes with black cave openings in them, lava flows, cinder cones, Glass Mountain—a high slope of shining black obsidian. But mostly he photographed clouds and falling rain above the parched land. We had our first experience of skid-chain installation when, halfway across a migratory-bird refuge lake on a narrow dike road, we came to otherwise impassable mudholes. Soft rain fell; geese, herons, and pheasants came out of the reeds below the dike to watch us wriggle about in the sloppy mud as we tried to adjust the chains.

October sixth, for the first time since we had left San Francisco, we woke up to a blue and cloudless sky. Tarpaulin, sleeping bags, blankets, clothes, were spread in the sun; haircuts exchanged; Heimy cleaned out. Heimy had been carrying an extra passenger for several days—a mouse, who had taken up residence between the back seat and the luggage compartment. Not having foreseen this possibility, Mr. Ford had made no provision for opening up this sanctuary; and because of the nightly rains we had been unable to lure our guest out by removing the foodstuff and leaving the doors open.

As we drove west through the mountains, Mt. Shasta dodged in and out of view, growing larger and higher with each reappearance, until we came around directly under its bow. I think it is only the Californian's love of superlatives that allows him to mention Mt. Whitney, while dwelling in the same state with Mt. Shasta. Whitney's claim to distinction is merely that it is the highest peak in the continental United States. As a mountain it is nothing to look at: just one of the many granite tips nearly as high that make up the imposing east wall of the Sierra. Shasta—but a few hundred feet shorter of stature—rises grand and solitary above a vast volcanic plain, dominating the landscape for a hundred miles. (No one would experience the slightest difficulty in picking it out while driving by in a car!) Shasta, then, is the real thing, whereas Whitney, after all, is only a mountain's mountain.

Our first act on reaching Yreka that afternoon was to march on a drygoods store and purchase two suits of long woolen underwear. (In the Lava Beds we had both worn three shirts and three pairs of sox simultaneously, though Edward had not sunk to my degraded practice of keeping pajamas on under my clothes throughout the day.) In front of a little movie house, a poster advertised, "BORNEO—*Martin Johnson's last picture.*"

"Oh, animals! Let's stay and see it."

"All right. Good chance to get rid of the mouse, too."

With such excuses to conceal our yearning for the luxury of hot showers, a warm clean room, dry wood to burn in an airtight stove, we disembarked at an auto-camp. Turned out Borneo wasn't showing till the next night, but we went in anyway to witness a stirring Class B epic of the deep south: Sharecroppers were ground under the heel of a low-down tyrant who was abetted by his villainous sister, until a clean-cut wholesome young newspaper reporter came to town, made justice triumph, in spite of a tense moment when a mob of sharecroppers—fooled into thinking he was on the other side—almost succeeded in lynching him; but just in the nick of time the daughter of the good sharecropper drove up and said: "He didn't hit me, the Wicked Sister did."

I don't know what we expected from the Klamath River road. We had heard it was beautiful country, and it was—a wild river canyon, narrow, steep-sided, heavily wooded and underbrushed. We looked down through gaps in the trees to the greenish-brown water in its channel of grey and white stones. There were a few settlements, isolated cabins, now and then a skimpy orchard. A primitive area, almost untouched by logging or other forms of civilization. But it was not a photographer's road or a photographer's landscape: there was too much underbrush, uninteresting growth—too little variety of form or texture.

It is the disadvantage of traveling with a photographer, that you become accustomed to looking at things from a photographic viewpoint. Once I would have rejoiced at the rich upholstery of underbrush, the unsettled land, the untracked mountains, the untamed river. Now, in spite of myself, I found the day-long negativeless drive down the winding river canyon monotonous. The only moment of excitement came when we passed a State Patrolman standing by his car in the road, calling to someone out of sight up the hill, "Get your hat and come on out." Constructing theories and counter-theories, we worked over the possibilities of that situation all the way to the coast.

So here we are again at Moonstone Beach, and, to remind us of Willard, here comes one of that homely kitten trio, mewing up to our campfire to see if by any chance we still carry Family Size steaks. Good weather reigns for a day and a half during which we swim in the river channel, lie on the great silver redwood logs in the sun, watch the gulls and pelicans that congregate on the wet sand at sunrise and sunset. Here, and on Little River Beach just across the channel, Edward photographs drift logs, bird- and bug-tracks on the sand, one junkpile with a heap of clam shells and a white metal doll buggy, another with an old shoe and a bean can.

When the sky turned threatening we dashed on south to the redwoods. Near Arcata we found a sign fit to companion the Sulphur Mines one in Red Rock Canyon. This said: 11,000 FEET TO MA'S HAMBURGERS. Again our unseasonalness was a blessing. The redwoods were deserted. In the Dyerville Grove where we made camp there was plenty of wood to burn, and, of course, a charming black and grey kitten—promptly christened Burleigh—came purring to meet us. We strung up the tarpaulin between an upended table and a couple of trees, making an open-sided cave whose sloping roof ended directly before the double-decker fireplace.* Thus we were warm and dry at once when the rain came, and since we did our cooking on the gas stove, Burleigh found warm sleeping quarters in the top compartment of the fireplace.

Ever since reading the childhood stories that began, "Once upon a time a wood-cutter and his son lived at the edge of a dark and gloomy forest," this is what I have thought a real forest should look like—giant trees with branches closing high overhead, cutting off the light; years of fallen needles carpeting the ground; moss-covered trunks lying here and there, hanging gardens of ferns and flowers growing from their upturned roots. The line of memorial groves south of Dyerville is preserved in its natural state; nothing is cleaned up or cut away. The gloomy shafts of the redwood trunks rise from a jungle of undergrowth—carpets of redwood sorrel, trillium, wild violets, ferns and mosses, as well as the multitudes of infant redwoods.

Edward was pleased that the sky remained overcast, since it meant no spotty patches of sunlight filtering through; but it was so dark under the trees that he could hardly see to focus, and ten-minute exposures were not uncommon. Although rain fell gently for most of the three days we spent there, the thick forest roof made such

*Many of the State Parks and Forest Service camps have two-compartment stone fireplaces: the large lower compartment for warmth-fire; the shallow, iron-topped, upper compartment for cooking fire.

an excellent umbrella that we often didn't know it was raining until we drove out into the open.

Burleigh saw us off in the mornings, welcomed us back to camp at night, purred like an airplane motor whenever we were around. He had so endeared himself that parting was a dreadful wrench. We had to call in cold reason, remember that he was fat and healthy on our arrival so hunting must be good here, that there was a little settlement across the bridge if he got too hungry or cold. Homeless wanderers that we were, we could offer him nothing half so good as his forest home. We put the remains of the last night's stew on a paper, put him in the top of the fireplace with it so he wouldn't see us drive away, and dashed off down the highway feeling like criminals.

North of Garberville the rain stopped and the sun shone out through hurrying clouds. From the edge of a bluff above the south fork of the Eel River we looked down on fields and trees, buildings and fences sparkling with raindrops. If Edward comments at all on newly made negatives, he is likely to be depreciative. When I have looked on the ground glass and commented enthusiastically, he will say, "I think it's all right," or, "It's not bad." Only when he is excessively pleased with the take—as when the last Eel River negative had been made—does he go so far as to say, "Think I got something that time!"

After that it was rain and more rain. We had to keep to the Redwood Highway all the way to Ukiah because the northern crossroads connecting with the coast were washed out or under repair. When we did get to the coast, roadwork plus rain gave us miles of taffy mud to drive through. Occasionally the downpour fell off for an hour and Edward jumped out to work. He did hills and ranches shrouded in drifting mist, a still little lagoon at the mouth of Alder Creek, grey shacks on the sea bluff. By the time we reached Duncan's Point, the force of the storm was broken, and Edward had a good morning of thick foam curdling over the rocks, rolling up in whipped cream layers on the dark beach.

Then the fog came in, so we started the last lap back to base. For the fifth time we looked at the chicken-coop hill, and although it was not at all as we had first seen it—recumbent cows were now mixed in with the chickens—Edward made a negative. Last stop was Tomales Bay where the sunset light turned the mudflats to sparkling diamond fields through which ran gleaming metallic rivers. Of the 149 films we had set out with three weeks before, only two were carried home unexposed.

10 New Mexico and Arizona

NOVEMBER, the rangers had told us, was the best month in Death Valley. We had planned to play a return engagement accordingly, but there was so much to do when we got back to the Los Angeles base that December was with us before we were ready to leave. At which point came a letter offering us a rent-free house near Santa Fe for a month; so, overnight, we shifted plans and set out December seventh for New Mexico.

After a month of urban existence, it was good to be on the road again—to be wearing comfortable old clothes, eating as we drove, caring neither what time it was nor where we would be tomorrow. And after a summer and fall in the north, it was good to be once more in the simplified geography of the desert. Crossing the Mojave on US 66, Edward specialized in abandoned service stations. Why are there so many of these desolate ruins dotted along the bleak shore of the desert? Does the enterprise fail for lack of water, or because the owners cannot endure the solitude, or because the modern automobile—carrying more gas and using less—no longer has need of half-way houses?

In some places fire was the obvious reason for abandonment: a lone chimney stood at the roadside, among piles of old shoes, broken dishes, and twisted torsos of rusty cars. But in others, everything had been left as if the people meant to return: tools in the shed, furniture in the house, even food on the table—while outside the desert wind sandblasted the building, blew the sagging door from its hinges, and passing motorists used the electric globes around the sign for target practice.

In the collection of wreckage we examined the first day, Edward was most delighted by the black and white pattern on the peeling top of an ancient car. (As an illustration of how fast automobile history moves, most people can't guess what this is, even with a part of the rear window opening thrown in for clue.) Early morning of the second day brought us to a deserted halfway house calling itself Siberia (here midsummer temperatures linger around 120°), where a giant white cup labeled HOT COFFEE stood in splendid isolation among the greasewood bushes. We stopped in Amboy to look again at the lot full of dilapidated carnival wagons we had seen in the spring; drove into the yard to find a man putting the finishing touches to a thorough job of renovation. You might return to a hundred desert junkyards, or a thousand, without finding a parallel. We gaped in disbelief; the man looked questioningly at us; we waved cheerily; he waved dubiously; we backed hastily out of the yard and returned to the highway.

For a long space there was neither ruin nor active settlement. A bare desert basin, studded evenly with greasewood, dark slopes growing pallid evil-looking forests of cholla cactus. A coyote stood by the road to watch us pass; when I backed Heimy for a better look, he stood his ground until we were opposite, then loped slowly off through the bushes.

That afternoon we crossed the Colorado River and entered Arizona, where the first sign said, SPEED LIMIT: PLEASE DRIVE CAREFULLY. At the quarantine station in Kingman, we asked the inspector what kind of weather was indicated. (The sky had been clouding over all afternoon.) A Californian would have replied at length—beginning with the fact that the cloudiness was most unusual for this time of year, going on to what had happened the previous year at this time, winding up with an exhaustive prediction. The Arizonan summed up briefly, "I've only lived here thirty-five years and I don't know a damned thing about the weather."

We were hurrying cross-country to take over our New Mexican residence on schedule; if there were snowstorms ahead we might have had to abandon US 66 for a longer southern route—hence our concern with the weather and our failure to take the side road up to the Grand Canyon. Northern Arizona rushed by Heimy's windows un-Westoned save for a half dozen negatives of clouds over distant mesas and the Painted Desert.

In New Mexico we returned to our old travel habits to this extent: when we found ourselves on the wrong road out of Albuquerque we stayed on it, pursuing a roundabout course to Santa Fe. North of Moriarty we followed a pink gravel road, hedged by barbed-wire fences stuck full of tumbleweeds, up a wide flat valley. The sky above us was clogged with clouds, so we drove in a dark storm shadow, but off to the left the clouds were broken into horizontal bands and a little sun was shining through on the world. A cold biting wind whipped down on us when Edward got out to make a negative, and the only car we saw on that road came by at sixty miles an hour spraying us and the camera with dust and gravel.

We were reminded of Los Angeles when a sign appeared, SANTA FE CITY LIMIT, and there was nothing in sight but hills and junipers and mountains. But presently we were passing some terribly artistic adobes, then winding through the narrow streets, the complex human and vehicular traffic, of Santa Fe in the throes of Christmas shopping. Ernie and Gina Knee (photographer and painter respectively) had just built a new adobe in Tesuque, six miles out of Santa Fe, and since that was also the whereabouts of the house we were looking for, we stopped to call and ask if they knew where it was.

Just stopped in for a moment, and, in best Guggenheim tradition, stayed ten days. First, it was too dark that night, they weren't sure where the place was, so better wait for daylight. Next day we found the house, but the owner was absent, so we left a note. Next day he informed us he wouldn't be leaving for a day or two. Finally we learned that he and his wife were divorcing, the house was community property, not his to dispose of in the first place. Meanwhile, expecting from day to day to move into quarters of our own, we were royally housed and fed at the Knees', and photography proceeded as usual.

The adobe was a mansion of ten or twelve rooms; besides Ernie and Gina, the family consisted of four Welsh terriers, whose favorite pastime was chasing stones. If you refused to come out and throw them, "Mr. Jones" would keep bringing them hopefully to the doorstep, until at last you would open the door to step out on a monumental rock pile.

On the morning of December 14th we woke up to find the world turned white. Edward—who had not photographed snow since his Chicago boyhood—went dashing out with his camera to spend a couple of fruitful hours on the objects around the house: the bed of tiny cactus plants with the loop of garden hose beside it, the wheelbarrows, the woodpile, the sawhorses, the iron garden bench—all were transformed into new shapes, given new meanings, by their delicate overlayers of white. Then we journeyed farther afield to find old sunflower stalks capped with snow, a river bottom lined with snow-draped trees—where Edward made a Currier & Ives—and a little ranch with a snow-lined fence and feathery trees against the dull grey sky. Each time we returned to the car it was festooned with a new crop of icicles.

Our second skid-chain bout occurred on the way up to Aspen Valley in the mountains back of Tesuque. This time it was Ernie's car—as badly designed for the purpose as ours—and it was deep soft snow we must mush around in for half an hour before we got the chains affixed. Frozen-fingered and -footed, we plowed on up to the summit to look across at a mountainside smoky with leafless aspens, a veil of snow clouds in the sky above it.

We had been looking for good aspens all year, and here they were in rich abundance. Edward did a grove of pale young trees against a dark hill with a miniature forest of dry grasses in the snow before it; he did forests of pole-like trunks—with their strange dark "eyes" spotted over the bark—against delicate cross shadows of the trunks on the snowy hillside; and farther down, below the snow line, white trunks rising from the dark slope to spread branches that held a last handful of withered leaves against a sky of flame-like clouds.

Edward had developed his east-bound negatives in Ernie's darkroom, so now we laid out a tour of places and people to see that would get us back to the Los Angeles base in good time for developing the balance. On Christmas Eve we arrived in Taos. My first surprise—Edward had been here before—was seeing Indians wandering around the plaza wrapped in the same kind of cotton wool blankets we used for sheets in our sleeping bags. My second, going into an eating place to find the same kind of arty tearoom that keeps the tourists happy in Carmel or Laguna Beach —colored glasses, woven napkins, flickering candles, conversation modulated to a refined hum. But here the scene was enlivened, as we waited for our food, by a big black dog who wandered about sweeping decorations from the tables with his waving tail, knocking ornaments off the Christmas tree and making a pretense, at least, of eating them. He had almost succeeded in tripping a waitress and bringing down a couple of indignant patrons, all in one masterly triple play, when it was discovered he belonged to no one within, and he was forthwith hustled out into the falling snow.

Early Christmas morning we drove up Taos Canyon, making first tracks in the fresh fall of powdery snow, Edward photographing dark little next-year's Christmas trees on the smooth white hills. Gina had told us to look up the Lockwoods in Taos, and there Edward found a rooftop of riches. He pointed the 8x10 down at the spouting pools of the State Fish Hatchery; up at the tracery of the leafless branches of a Chinese elm against the dark sails and vane of a windmill; over the streets and buildings of Taos where, in the distance, a tiny white cross on the roof of a church was outlined against the dark mountains.

Most New Mexico roads look as though they had been laid out with ruler and pencil in a New York office; with apparent disregard for topographical features, they persistently follow the course that was once considered to be the shortest distance between two points. If the road meets a ridge of hills, instead of wandering off to find an easy grade, it shoots straight up this side, drops straight down the other. As we drove south to Albuquerque Edward made a negative of one of these long straight ribbons of highway. (When it was later published in the *New Mexico Maga-*

NEW MEXICO AND ARIZONA

zine, the editors showed their sense of delicacy by performing a Caesarean section on the print to remove the wrecked car in the foreground.)

We spent three days with Willard Nash in a hundred-and-fifty-year-old adobe near Albuquerque. Except for the room Willard painted and slept in, the place was bare of furniture or fixtures; so we made indoor camp in one of the large empty rooms, spreading our sleeping bags on the rough board floor in front of a noble fireplace. The fortress construction of the building had been little tampered with: the rooms enclosed, and opened into, a small square patio; the outside walls, for the most part, remained pure of windows, gun loopholes supplying their only openings. What had probably begun as a stable and evolved to a garage was now a catch-all chamber littered with incongruous junk. Edward found that on his first inspection tour, then settled down to work on details of the crumbling adobe walls, interspersed with pictures of me sun-bathing in the weed-grown patio. We celebrated New Year's Eve by heating buckets of water and bathing—after a fashion—in front of a roaring fire.

All New Year's Day we drove south through New Mexico under a gloomy grey sky; the following day, turned west under a gloomier one, our road paralleling a railroad with lonesome little stops named, FLORIDA, TUNIS, MONGOLIA, LISBON. Before Lordsburg, where the southern and northern routes across Arizona diverge, we saw our first competitive highway advertising. The southern route was recommended three times by large billboards advising the motorist to avoid miles of mountains and desert waste by taking US 80 through beautiful Tucson, etc. But the burden of their argument was competently undermined by a multitude of impertinent little red signs posted at hundred-yard intervals, saying on behalf of US 70: TRAVEL 70. MOUNTAINS 70. SCENERY 70. HUNTING 70. FISHING 70. COOLIDGE DAM 70. COTTON 70. WARM 70. COOL 70. HOT 70. COLD 70. COMFORT 70. CONTENTED 70.

Happily, we had already elected to follow 70 as the most direct route to our next stop-off, Prescott. I can't vouch for all of the attractions specified in that list, but Coolidge Dam alone would have been sufficient inducement. We arrived at dusk on a point overlooking the impounded waters of the dam, San Carlos Lake by name. Below us, at the base of a hillside of spiny brush and prickly pear, little crab-claw points extended into the smooth water; across the pale vacant surface of the lake, the far shoreline was broken by dark reflections of the speckled mountains that piled up in the distance. The violent contrast of elements—the age of nature's desert mountains, the shiny newness of man's lake—gave the somber landscape a disquieting aspect of unreality; as though a mirage had momentarily come to life, but might at any moment fade before our eyes.

In Prescott we stayed five days with the Sommers: Frederick (painter and photographer), Frances, and their two eye-dropper-raised cats, Ricky (for rickets) and Micky (for rhyme). Prescott, five-thousand-and-some feet up in the mountains, is strategically located, with roads radiating from it in all directions. The variety of country round about was compensation for the weather which—to us sissy Californians—was cold far past the bracing point.

On the afternoon we were driving back from Skull Valley Edward found a skull set on a fence post, and with little light and long exposures made several variations of it. He then insisted I must index the negatives as made in Skull Valley. I pointed out that there weren't twenty-nine palms at Twentynine Palms, there wasn't a lone pine at Lone Pine, nor a dead man at Deadman's Point—so to go around bragging that we'd found a skull in Skull Valley would be flying in the face of established tradition. Edward conceded the point grudgingly and the negatives were indexed as made on the Iron Springs Road. Another day we found a charming home-made sign on the Cherry Creek Road, pointing to the Quarter-Circle-V-Bar Ranch, and saw a cliff dwelling called Montezuma's Castle which had nothing whatever to do with Montezuma.

But the prize in the Prescott region is Jerome. A copper town built on the vertical face of a mountain, its streets are precipices, its buildings stand on each other's heads. Frances told us they mined no longer—the smelter down in the valley was the town's only source of employment. But in the bygone mining days, they had tunnelled into the mountain under the town so extensively, that now and then a cave-in occurs and one or two houses slip from A-street down to B-street. Frances also passed on the local legend that children who grew up in Jerome walked all their lives—wherever they might be—at a 45° angle.

When we came out on an open turn of the mountain road to look down on the town, it was half hidden in the yellow-grey smoke from the smelter. However, Edward set to work with gusto, while I recorded for posterity the sign at the side of the road:

YOU ARE NOW ENTERING

JEROME ARIZONA

THE MOST UNIQUE TOWN

IN AMERICA

ONE MILE HIGH

FIFTY MILE VIEW

—Jerome Chamber of Commerce

Well, it was time to be getting home now. Good-bye to the Sommers, good-bye to Prescott, good-bye to Arizona. But first a day of Saguaros on the Aguila Cut-off: not the pristine fluted columns that Edward had done around Phoenix, but monstrous pillars of ruin, totem poles of decay. And first, a final mystery to bind us to the state of Arizona by invisible threads of speculation and questioning. Who is the *Yuma Nymph?* How came she there? A life-size silver statue of a naked Indian maiden holding on high a silver bowl from which sprouts a (real) niggerhead cactus. Shining and solitary she stands on a desert plain, against a backdrop of distant mountains. While Edward made two negatives, I examined a glass-topped case near by, which contains petrified beets, turnips, potatoes, wood, and a piece of tablet paper covered with pencil writing:

These petrified vegetables are souvenirs of the Desert. The petrified garden where these vegetables are found lies about 1800 feet from here. They were planted perhaps several millions years ago. By a forgotten people, that once inhabited this country. The ferns on these vegetables are preserved by nature through millions of years. These souvenirs are for sale at the house. And if you wish to go over to the garden I will show you. We do not charge you.

The little farmhouse was not far off. My impulse was to go clear up the mystery at once; but it was late, we wanted to get to Blythe that night and home the next day because Edward's exposed films had stayed too long undeveloped. The statue was right on the highway—lots of people would know all about it; so we moved on, darkness descended on the desert, the moon came up to light the silver ribbon of the Colorado, and we were back on California soil. In two years of inquiry, all I have learned about the mysterious nymph is this: because she stands between two bends in the highway, most Arizona-California commuters drive by so fast they don't even see her.

11 Borrego, Yosemite, and Death Valley II

As the first taste of human blood is said to affect certain of the larger carnivorous quadrupeds, so with Edward and the taste of snow we had had in New Mexico. He must have more, and immediately. We were packed and ready to depart for Yosemite Valley when Ansel wired saying "no snow," so we removed our long woolies from the clothes bag, drained off Heimy's anti-freeze, and turned south for a look at Borrego State Park.

We took the Palms to Pines Highway (route of return from Salton Sea last spring) in reverse, to look again at the speckled mountainside that Edward still remembered as a good opportunity missed. But alas for returnings: what had been in the spring a glittering medley of young green agaves, scarlet-tipped ocotillos, and dry white agave stalks against the black rocks was reduced in the winter to a single-toned, drab mass, with the dusty grey plants fading into the dry earth. The highway provided compensation, however, in the form of a jolly flying horse, who looked as if he had seen service on a merry-go-round before he was set in the sky to call attention to a dude ranch.

We had two good days of concretions (and date milkshakes) before a windstorm chased us off the Salton plain, up into Borrego Valley and the rain. No matter. We had come to like our weather virile. If the sun stayed out indefinitely the 8x10 would probably cease to function, so long had it been nurtured on swift successions of sun and rain, windstorms and dense fog, sea spray and snow. Before we had even pitched the tent, Edward had the camera set up in the persisting drizzle, aimed at the delicate arch of rainbow that stood over valley and hill.

In Borrego, as in the Lava Beds, contrast is the keynote. Here is a crazy riot of badlands, an infinite sea of dry wrinkled mud cliffs (Edward said: "Come see! It's absolutely mad—they look right side up on the ground glass!"); and its next-door neighbor is a canyon of Washingtonia (native) palms, growing from the bed of a roaring mountain stream. And speaking of contrasts, there was a photographic one, beyond the scale of any film yet made: as in most of the easily accessible canyons, the palm grove had been fired by vandals, leaving the tapering trunks a grim charcoal-black, while the granite boulders that littered the stream bed had been polished by the mountain torrent to dazzling white.

That's about all we saw of Borrego, because then the rain came for keeps. We returned to base in a day-long downpour, stayed only long enough for developing, and moved on—taking Neil along—to Yosemite. On the Ridge Route Edward made negatives of the folded hills against a pall of wintry clouds. North through the long flat valley of the San Joaquin, from oil wells to cotton to grapes, to orchards of peach and fig, the rain increasing in force as we drove, and the wind rising.

California is inclined to soft-pedal any extreme manifestations of its weather, cherishing its reputation for climatic temperance. But there had been sufficient floods in December for us to read of them in the New Mexican newspapers, and now we saw some effects. The All Year Highway into Yosemite had had large bites taken out of it by the Merced River, which had also removed a good portion of the narrow-gauge tracks from the opposite canyon wall, and was now engaged in devouring the twisted loops of metal in its swirling rapids.

Ansel's last word had been that we'd better come along and take a chance; there might be snow and there might not. The rain that had accompanied us all the way followed us into the valley, where the peaks were hidden in grey mist and the ground was covered with grey slush. Virginia and Ansel welcomed us with pessimistic views of the weather in prospect: now that the rain had started it would likely keep on. Other Yosemiteans agreed: another snowfall was not indicated, because, etc., etc.

That was Wednesday, the ninth of February. During the night the rain turned to snow and for two more days and nights the white stuff came down without inter-ruption. Elsewhere in the state the weather was even more vigorous. We clustered around the radio to learn of a hurricane, no less, that had smashed windows in San Francisco, blown trees and houses down elsewhere, even produced a waterspout off Point Lobos. Then came the news that the All Year Highway was closed by slides, the telephone lines out of the valley were down—in short, we were cut off from the outside world. Romantic thought, indeed; but if no one had told us we wouldn't have noticed, since we had no intention of leaving and no desire to telephone.

When the sun came up in a blue sky Saturday morning, Edward went berserk. Everywhere he looked there was something to photograph: trees top-heavy with snow, buildings mantled with thick white over-roofs, wires built up with snow till they looked like tree branches. We dug Heimy out of his overstuffed union suit and went exploring. The roads that had been cleared were narrow canyons between the four- (or more) foot banks. Edward would call a halt when he saw something, indicate the direction he proposed to take; then Neil and I would lunge into the waist-deep whiteness, beating down a path for Edward to follow with camera and film-case. At the end of the trail we packed down a circle of snow so the tripod legs wouldn't go through to China, and Edward clipped his focussing cloth to the front of the camera to protect the bellows against occasional dumpings from the overhead branches.

For a week we pursued this cold wet system of athletics. The snowplows opened more roads each day, so there were always new places to see. Edward did cliffs and rocks, the fields and the river, icicles and snowbanks, the intricate networks of black and white branches. Avalanches of snow came thundering down from the cliff tops; vapory clouds formed on the peaks and went sailing off into the sky; when the sun had melted half the snow, there was another fall, and another. The road to the ski lodge at Badger Pass was cleared, and we had a day of really deep snow up on the mountain, where the road banks were over Heimy's head, and the little trees were cloaked white figures on the silent slopes. When we had plowed through the cold white world all day we would return, tired and half-frozen, to the campground de luxe of the Adams Studio—to hot baths, good food, a roaring fire, and warm comfortable beds. It was fun to indulge our pioneer spirit in the daytime, while looking forward to the civilized pampering evening would bring.

By the end of the week Edward was forced to admit he had had enough snow, for a while anyway. Might as well get on back to Los Angeles, to keep our long-deferred appointment with Death Valley. But first Los Angeles, then Death Valley, thought otherwise. We arrived at base, February 27th. It rained all night, most of the next day, and the next. By March second even the most conservative Southern Californian had to call a flood a flood. Canyons and valleys were inundated and cut off, all roads out of town were blocked, the radio was requesting people to stay home and not to use the telephone except for emergency. The lights went out so often we became accustomed to candles, and forgot to try the switch at all. A section a few blocks from our base was evacuated, and friends kept calling up to see if we needed a new home. We fretted and fumed to no avail. When the roads out of Los Angeles were passable all the roads into Death Valley were flooded or washed out. There was nothing for it but to sit home reading of the wreckage, listening to the radio accounts, waiting.

On such occasions the California rivers pay back for insult and belittlement. People laugh at them, make jokes about them, build their houses in dry washes and river beds. At last the river's patience is exhausted and in one mighty rush it sweeps down on the houses and bridges, carrying a welter of human foolishness out to sea. When the people come back to find their lots as well as their houses gone, you think they have learned a lesson. But a few dry years pass, the people forget; the old jokes are dragged out, the houses are rebuilt in the channels, the performance is repeated.

The roads were soon patched together; we left March seventh on the last trip of the Guggenheim year. It was strange to see the familiar desert roads banked by wide ditches of water, the dry lakes transformed to wet lakes, the scraped red and brown desert mountains capped with lacy snow. When we passed the checking station on Death Valley's western boundary, the ranger told us it had been raining off and on for a week, whereupon a gentle shower commenced, accompanied us across the valley and south to Furnace Creek.

Roughly speaking—and most unscientifically—the geographic plan of the Death Valley region is that of the state of California reduced in scale: a long, narrow valley, running northwest to southeast, enclosed by chains of high mountains. Photographically, the parallel can be carried another step; as Edward had found the least material to whet his negative appetite on the flat reaches of California's central valley, so he made few negatives here on the actual valley floor—it was the enclosing mountain ranges that provided photographic riches in subject matter and vantage points.

Opposite to the California scheme, Death Valley's higher mountain wall is in the west—the Panamints; the lower in the east—the Funerals. At a point about two-thirds down its length, the latter range is cut through by Furnace Creek Wash, and that junction may be considered (for all purposes but geographic) the center of the monument. First, the main settlement is there: Furnace Creek Inn stands at the mouth of the wash on the north side; Furnace Creek Ranch (cabins, store, date grove, etc.) on the north side of the gravel fan that spreads out from the wash.

Second, there lies on the south side of the wash at this point, a triangular area of badlands containing some of the most spectacular scenery in the monument. On two sides of the triangle the gullied mud-hills rise from the levels of the wash and the valley floor, to roll back in higher and higher ranks until the third side melts into the dark rocky mountains to the south. This is the domain of pure erosion. The forms of the mud-hills have the clarity and precision of textbook diagrams. There is almost unlimited variety of shape, pattern, texture, and color. Each hill you climb gives a new accounting of the complex intertexture of cliffs, hills, ridges, gullies, sumps, and dry falls. About half of all Edward's Death Valley negatives were made in that comparatively small section; half of all our Death Valley days were passed in clambering up and down the puffy clay hills, cutting steps as we progressed along the knife-edged pebbly ridges, looking for new viewpoints, or returning to old ones to see things in different light. From the four roads that penetrate the area (20-Mule Team Canyon, Corkscrew Canyon, Zabriskie Point, and Golden Canyon) we blazed our own foottrails over the whole wasteland, until we had climbed at least every other mud-hill in the triangle.

The Texas Springs campground is set back in a fold of mud-hills on a bench above the Ranch. The mesquite trees that had been feathery green the year before were transformed on our second coming to leafless brown skeletons whose scraggly branches underlined the barrenness of the baked clay flat from which stone tables and faucets rose at suitable intervals. There were more campers now—the coveted sites on the periphery were all taken, so we had to content ourselves with a less-protected central position. For the first few days of clouds and occasional light showers, that made no difference; but on the fourth day the wind began, and from then on we were never without it for more than a day at a time.

Ordinarily three days of blow would have sufficed to send us packing, but from New Mexico, application had gone to the Guggenheim Foundation for a second year (half photographing, half printing), and we had pledged ourselves to remain in Death Valley until the answer came. So we must stay and make the best of the worst weather yet encountered. The tentpole snapped in the first day's blow; we braced it with splints, bound it with wire, tied ropes from the four roof corners to neighboring mesquites. Most nights the pole creaked so ominously and the canvas walls flapped so violently, we expected the roof to fall on us every moment; but our crude repair job held and we rode out all subsequent gales.

We had a varied succession of neighbors in the campground. One night we would drop off to sleep to a heated discussion of Hitler, the man (*What is he Really like?*), from which one set of famous last words stands out vividly, "Of course, you're entitled to your opinions, and I'm willing to concede that you're 75% right, *but* . . . ." Another night it would be two Englishmen, standing by their monster trailer, seriously arguing the question of whether Americans call Orion "The Dipper." One morning the shrill complaint of a woman to her neighbor awakened us: "Ahm cehtunly goin' to write mah daughtah an' tell heh not to come heah. Ah wanted to take mah dog foh a walk and pick wild flowahs; instead they's such a wind it almost blew mah trailah ovah. Ah'd leave heah right now but they's such a duststoam ah couldn't get mah trailah ovah the

162   Iron Springs Road / Arizona

166 Taos/from Lockwood's Roof

172   Columbia River Gorge / Oregon

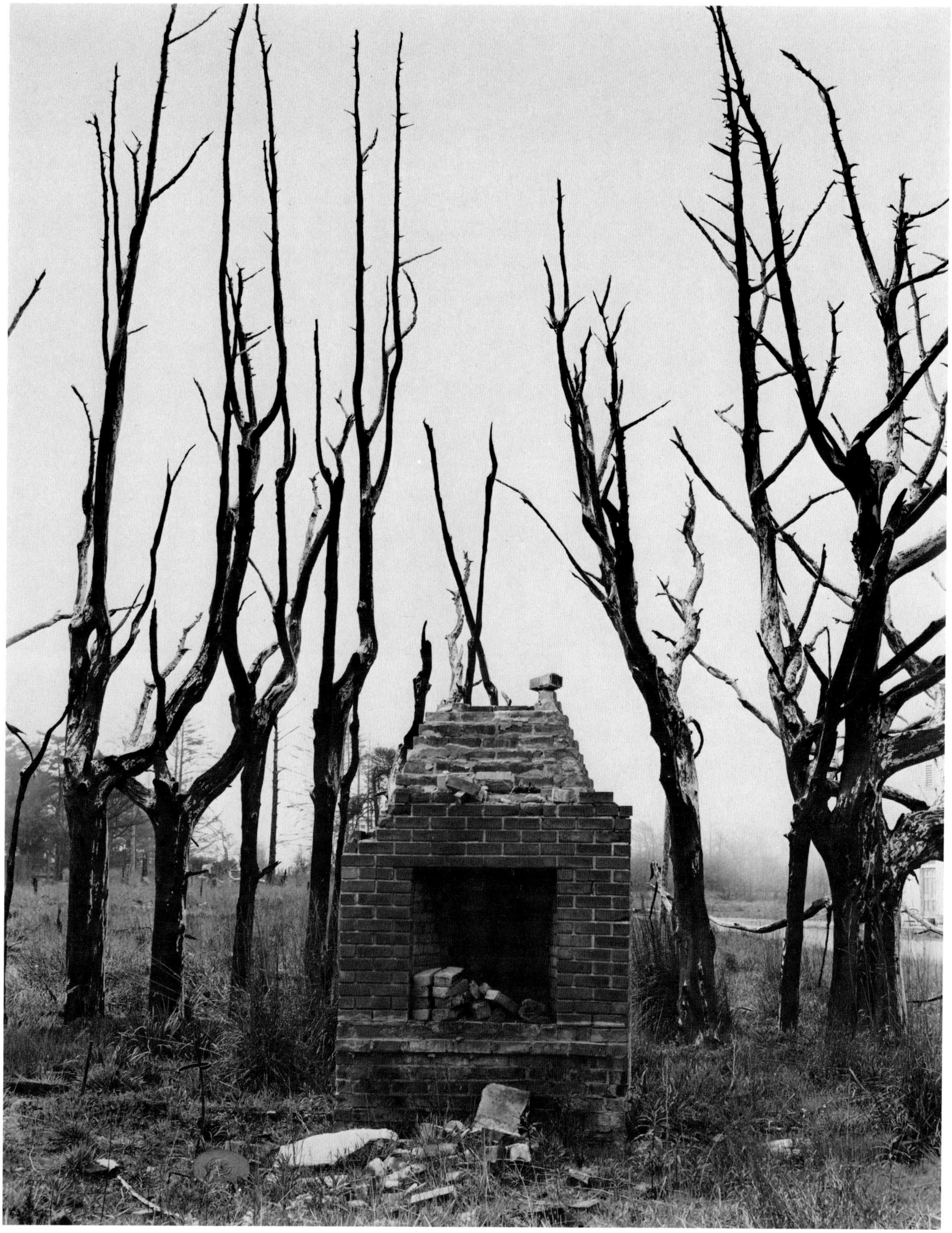

After Forest Fire / Bandon, Oregon

Panamints. Of cose, Death Valleh's rugged an' all that, but ah can't see why *enni-one* would come back heah a second time."

The Taylors were an old couple with a middle-aged dog, who lived in a 1925 Packard in the lot across from us. They cooked at the back of the car, slept inside it, and during the day sat on folding chairs with the middle-aged dog on one or the other lap. We took Mr. Taylor along to Golden Canyon one day. He wore baggy overalls, a battered hat, and a little wisp of chin beard. He told me he used to be a painter. One day he was painting in Central Park and the darn thing wouldn't come right, so he got mad, threw it down on the grass, kicked it along, went over and picked up the purtiest storm scene you ever saw. Then he did a portrait of a Wall Street financier. The man paid him five hundred dollars and said, "Taylor, you're a better salesman than you are a painter. Come on down to Wall Street and I'll see you make more money in a year than you would in ten at that stuff." And, bigosh, the man was right: he made ten thousand dollars in a year. But keeping a yacht was the way to lose money fast; his cost him fifty dollars a day to run, and it cost him twenty dollars every time he took his dog across Long Island—they wouldn't let it on the train so he had to go by taxi. His main trouble now was that his stomach didn't work so well; he had to use a pound of baking soda a week. His stomach always seemed to know when he got away from his baking soda, because right then it always started to ache. The Taylors had been back and forth across the country so many times I lost count. When they got to Salt Lake he wanted to swim, and his wife raised cain with him for not telling her sooner, because she didn't have her Annette Kellerman with her. They'd be moving on soon now. His feet were beginning to itch; and when they started itching it was time to get along. Didn't matter where they went so long as they moved on.

On a day that showed early promise of being clear and windless, we drove over Daylight Pass to Rhyolite in Nevada. Here is the western ghost town at its nakedest. Rhyolite's gold boom came in 1906; its death in 1907. The town was deserted and everything movable in it was carried away. Parts of the walls of a three-story hotel, a two-story bank, and a grocery face each other across a weed-bordered desert road. Sections of worn adobe wall rise here and there from the trash heaps of broken bottles, old shoes, rusty metal, and tin cans.

We had judged our weather wrong. A cold wind beat on us savagely from the moment of our arrival. I held the heavy tripod anchored while Edward worked to get the ruins against the pale storm clouds that were drifting up the sky. The town is set up on a slope of bare colored hills, and while Edward worked we could look down on an arm of the Amargosa Desert that was being rapidly transformed to a sea of blowing sand. Edward was fascinated with the town—Nevada's Athens, he called it—and would doubtless have found more to do in better weather. But there is a saturation point in a wind like this; after an hour of constant buffeting, or sand and gravel slapping into your face and eyes, you can't breathe and you can't see and you can't stand up any longer.

So we retired down the hill with seven negatives, with Heimy's windshield thoroughly pitted—with every intention of coming back on the first clear day. There weren't any really clear days after that. Death Valley filled up to the brim with blowing sand and alkali dust and did its best to stay that way. We went north in the valley to the dunes, where Edward photographed the grim mesquite skeletons that had been choked and buried by drifting sand, and unburied when the wind shifted. We went up in the Panamints for a day of cold wind, while Edward photographed windblown clouds over the peaks. We went back several times to Dantes View (the road had been surfaced all the way up, so now the trip was easy). The view itself had been completely transformed. The brilliant contrasts of the first year had been replaced by soft tones of liver and blue. The salt bed was covered by a thin sheet of water, that shrank in from the edge during our stay, exposing a widening margin of white salt.

A year before, Curry had given us our baptism of rugged desert driving. This year we accompanied him on an even wilder trip. The rock that had blocked the entrance to Copper Canyon had been blasted away the day before, so this was an historic event; we were in the first car to enter the canyon. We jolted up over a steep alluvial fan, the wheel tracks ended and the fun began. In its early stages the canyon was no more than a narrow passage between walls of pink rock—a steep, winding passage, bedded deep with gravel. Curry's car, a monster of high-slung body and big wheels, charged noisily forward, stuck, retreated, and charged again. Progress was painfully slow. The turns were so sharp and the walls shut in so close, it looked as though we would surely be smashed against them.

Every fibre of wood and molecule of metal shrieked protest as we jolted over boulders, plunged up dry rapids, rattled through loose rocks. In one arm of the canyon we came to rest in a circle of rocks so big you could reach out the window and pat their heads. It took Curry twenty minutes to turn the car which tipped up almost on its side before it came crashing down off the boulders. While we lunched in a wide bowl that opened out in mid-canyon, I climbed a little gully to look at the view, and brought down a slab of pink rock with amusing designs on it to show Edward. Curry looked at it and announced feelingly that he'd be a XxxX XxxX XxxX!, for these were some fine tracks of two-toed birds.

On days when the wind was at its worst we drove up to the turnaround on Zabriskie Point, to watch the passing human stream that Came and Saw and (usually) Clicked. There was a fat man in a dark blue business suit, champing a black cigar, who remarked to his wife after surveying the multicolored badlands, "Well, it's certainly booful; very booful." There was a man who came up frequently to survey the prospect through a viewing glass and remark to his patient wife, "Well, dear, nothing up here; let's go down below and see how it looks." One day a touring car with a Mexican license drove up. Three German couples piled out, with six cameras (one woman had none but one man had two). The five enthusiasts lined up, focussed on the same view, decided on the exposure, made the picture. Four of them lined up at the other side of the turnaround, made a second picture in unison. Then they climbed back in the car and drove away.

On the 27th of March the long-awaited letter came, and its news was good. We got dizzy unwinding the yards of wire from the tentpole, celebrated with a final swim in the pool. Weathered and windburned—Edward disguised in a three-weeks' beard—we headed back to base.

12 The Second Year

IN this account, the second year must come as an epilogue. Not that we didn't continue to travel, to see new places, to have more adventures—for we did all these things. But we had a home that second year, so everything was changed. When printing became the order of the day, we got out of the swing of our peripatetic existence, and the trips we made were sandwiched in more as vacations from harder work than as ends in themselves.

At first it seemed we could never settle down, there was so much of California yet to see. Edward would need a darkroom of his own for printing, and we might combine traveling and photographing with hunting for a nice old house that we could buy with the Guggenheim rent budget plus the renewed *Westways* contract. It goes without saying that such a course would have produced many more negatives than possible houses, but at this point the problem was settled for us by a letter from my father: "I have a good piece of ground going to waste across the canyon; why not come up here and build your own house?"

Well, why not? With the funds available we could compromise between the simplicity of camp life and the complexity of a normal dwelling, by having everything in one big room. Neil was a carpenter, we'd tell him what we wanted, and make a trip while he put it up. We moved our goods and chattels north, sat around the lamp one night drawing plans, left Neil pouring foundations, and departed for the Mother Lode.

My prophecy of the year before proved correct so far as the towns went; Edward found little to do. But the foothills were yellow again, the oaks were black against them, wild buckeye bloomed at the roadside, so the trip was not without issue. In spite of my warnings, Edward had been led to expect more ruins, and each sleepy little town we drove through was subjected to unfavorable comparison with Nevada's Athens.

At night we climbed up higher in the mountains to cool off. Once more we camped in the Maple Grove on the American River, above Placerville. The year before we had complained of the restricted bathing facilities; now the river had washed half the campground away and it still rushed by in a wide brown flood, topped with racing foam, filled with swirling rapids. Another night we camped in a grove of incense cedars just below the snow line on Carson Pass, and going down the mountain next morning Edward made his favorite Mother Lode negative, of the shiny charcoal surface of a burned stump at the roadside. The town of Volcano came nearest to having real ruins. There Edward was tempted to do three narrow arches in a rock wall; but they were mixed up with repair rails in front, and trees in back, and if he had never seen Rhyolite, etc. Outside of Ione we stopped to examine a large graveyard with signs erected on all the paths saying, *Please remove all your rubbish over the back fence.*

June ninth we arrived in Yosemite, and next day Ansel took us to Meyers Ranch, on the heights above the valley. The barns and outbuildings, weathered to a warm reddish brown, were set in a meadow of high green grass speckled with clover blossoms. Six varieties of fence went wandering here and there through the clearing; there was a big spoked wheel mounted on a shed—Ansel said it was an old slaughter wheel; little streams cut through the meadow; bleached white skulls and bones lay in the grass. We had arrived in sunshine, but dark clouds soon piled up over the pines and hilltops until the sky was blanketed over, and a strange moody light settled down on the old cattle ranch. Edward and Ansel photographed feverishly to be through before the rain came; while they worked I crawled about the pasture reaping a harvest of wild strawberries.

When we got back to base Neil had the darkroom finished, the rest of the house half done. Soon the last bat was in place and we moved in, finding it good to have a home again, fun to settle down and sprout roots. Edward, taking up the monumental task of printing the Guggenheim negatives, disappeared into the darkroom for days at a time. When he came up for air occasionally, we made short trips in the surrounding country; he photographed a pear orchard in the Carmel Valley and a barn near Salinas we had long admired. But mostly we spent our days-off at Point Lobos, only a mile from our front door.

Edward began by saying he was all through with it. (He'd been saying that ever since he left Carmel in 1935.) Hadn't he photographed there for six years, done every twisted cypress on the cliffs and every eroded rock on the beaches? True enough, but that had been a period of close-ups: details of rocks, fragments of trees. At first we just went out to swim and look at the scenery and walk; but Edward took his camera along in case he might see a cloud or something. He made a few negatives; we went oftener; he made more. Soon we were going out once a week and Edward was making more negatives than ever, most of them quite different from his earlier seeing of the same material. He did tide pools, landscapes, groves of cypress, seaweed and kelp in the water, breaking waves, and long views of the rugged shoreline. In the summer there was fog drifting over the rocky inlets; in the fall there were big storms to churn the foam up on the dark rocks.

So the months passed in making new negatives almost as fast as the old ones were printed, and December was with us before we set out on another long trip. We spent fifteen more days in Death Valley, where for the first time we had a long spell of clear weather, followed by a three-day rainstorm that nearly washed us out of the campground but provided Edward with magnificent clouds.

Then we went back to Los Angeles to make a trip that had been projected for two years past—a tour through the storage lots of Metro-Goldwyn-Mayer. When arrangements had been made (thanks to Cedric Gibbons and Warren Newcombe), we arrived on a most unpromising day. Culver City was wrapped in a tule fog; the sky was blank white and sunless. But no such minor consideration stopped Edward once he discovered the fantastic world that lay within.

It began with the pond on Lot One. The white painted side-wheeler, "Maria Theresa" (*The Great Waltz*), was drawn up to a dock at one end; a row of small boats beached at the other end made foreground for a meticulously painted flat of the Marseilles waterfront (*Port of Seven Seas*). On Lot Two there were whole blocks of stairways stacked together, leading to nowhere. On Lot Three stood the remains of a huge ballroom (*Rosalie*), a forest of oil derricks on the distant hills showing between the ornate white pillars and the naked wooden skeletons of ornamental trees. While Edward was working there, some workmen drove up in a truck and set a post-hole driller going in the middle of the ballroom floor. Warren Newcombe, who was making the rounds with us, strolled over to ask what they were doing; came back to report they had to string some ropes up so the monkeys could practice jumping for *Tarzan*.

At the far corner of Lot Three, among assorted statues, we found a group of three that surpassed all the rest: Marianne, white and heroic; Lincoln, pensive and medium-sized; and a small, one-armed football player—all tied by the neck with stout ropes. After lunch we returned to Lot One to explore the byways around the pond. Among the braces that held up some building fronts, Edward found three carved figureheads. I was sure they were real waterworn wood until I had gone up to touch them. But after all I was a newcomer, and Warren—who had seen such perfect imitations made for years—admitted that he still had to go up and thump things occasionally to see if they weren't just possibly what they seemed to be.

Toward the end of the day I found an open shelf filled with rubber dummies, above one of stuffed horses. When Edward had made a negative I pulled one of the dummies out. He was a heavy creature, of dark, spongy rubber, with a cast face that was unnervingly realistic. From the top of his head protruded a bit of wire which we supposed must be used to hang him up for dressing. Next I pulled out a greenish-yellow one. The first had stood up straight as a ramrod, but the second, having a fractured leg, settled into a more elastic pose, that demanded the exposure of the day's last film.

Two months later we made our farewell tour, going north to Vancouver, returning by the coast. In Vancouver, Seattle, and most of Washington, visibility was as zero as it had ever been in a fog on the California coast, or a duststorm on the desert. We had arrived in the spring burning season, when people of the north clear their land, burn rubbish and stumps, against the fire-hazard months of summer. For a week we traveled around under a grey pall of smoky fog that kept Edward's negative output to the minimum. But in Oregon things picked up a little with an exciting morning on the Columbia River Highway, where we looked down Dantes View-fashion on the wide gorge with its island of green trees and fields.

Whenever in the past two years we had mentioned the delights of the California north coast, someone had always been on hand to say, "If you like that, wait till you see the Oregon coast." So we expected great things, and were disappointed. Unlike the California coast road (*not* to be confused with the Redwood Highway) which is seldom out of sight of the ocean, the Oregon "coast road" strays frequently, and for long periods, inland among uninteresting forests of second-growth pine. When it does get out to the coast proper, no one could ask for better treatment. There are logs on the beaches California style—Edward did one at sunset with fog rolling in on the water, windblown trees on the steep cliffs, new bridges and old towns.

One memorable day we came out to the coast in thick fog to drive between rows of ghostly chimneys, white skeletons of buildings, black skeletons of trees. That was Bandon, burned in a forest fire two years before. The fog stayed with us all the next day, so Edward photographed it, with a little bit of Cape Sebastian showing through. At Crescent Beach we wandered around in more fog, looking for the logs of 1937. Edward hadn't expected to work but he found a wrecked car that needed doing and a stump to end all stumps.

We spent three more days in the redwoods, revisited some of the coast towns, turned inland to Clear Lake. Nearing it, we stopped by a small, tree-lined pond called Blue Lake, opposite a man who was working on a road machine. Edward got out to look at the reflections in the water and the man said, "Sure is a pretty lake, isn't it?" We agreed, and he retired into the bowels of the machine to do some tinkering. A second car stopped, and two men—one with a Leica on his chest—climbed out to examine the view. In a moment a voice issued from the depths of the road machine, "Sure is a pretty lake, isn't it?" The man busy with his Leica said "Yes"—then realizing we hadn't spoken and his companion hadn't spoken, began to look around for the voice, saying, "But where did it come from?"

"Oh, it's always been there," came the reply from the road machine.

We had a day of warm sunshine at Clear Lake. The redbud was blooming along the highway, and when we climbed up a hill road, Edward made a negative looking down on green fields and sheep with the lake and mountains beyond.

Then we turned out to the coast for the last time, and came to the perfect setting of vineyards we had always hoped to find. While Edward set up, a road scraper came relentlessly down the highway toward us, manufacturing a continuous duststorm as it advanced. But whether for reasons of roadwork or kindness of heart, the man turned his machine before the dustcloud got abreast of us; and the negative Edward hadn't made, on the first stop of the first trip, was at last brought into the fold.

A Statement by Edward Weston

THE PROJECT: In explaining the nature of the project I carried out under a two-year Guggenheim Fellowship (1937-39), I can do no better than begin with the question I have answered one thousand (1000) times in the last three years—"Do all these photographs you have made belong to the Guggenheim Foundation?" The answer is no. Applicants for Guggenheim Fellowships submit their own projects. The Guggenheim Foundation grants awards (on the basis of thorough preliminary investigation) to enable the recipients to carry out their chosen projects; the Foundation asks nothing in return.

Such a Fellowship enabled me, for two years, to devote full time to the kind of photography that had formerly, of necessity, been relegated to spare time. Further, it enabled me to put one of my pet theories to test in actual practice. Photography has long been considered a mass-production medium from the standpoint of unlimited duplication of prints. But that is a factory job, requiring standardization and mechanicalization beyond the scope of the individual who uses photography as a creative expression. Not the mass-production of duplication, but the possibility for "mass-production" of original work, is, I have long felt, one of photography's most important potentialities for the artist.

Unlike other mediums of expression that demand a greater or lesser expending of time for the realization of original vision, the actual making of a photograph is accomplished, so to speak, in a moment. Not as a writer makes notes for future elaboration into a story, not as a painter makes sketches that will be later worked into a picture: not the idea, suggestion, but the whole picture is made on the instant. So nearly do conception and execution coincide, they may be said to be simultaneous. Of course that is the negative; the print—the form in which the picture will be seen—remains to be made. But that is only a matter of carrying out the complete original vision as represented by the negative; it can be done ten minutes later or ten years.

It goes without saying that in order to work in this fashion, the photographer must be complete master of his tools and processes; he must be so familiar with their potentialities and limitations that his seeing will be automatically translated into the physical facts of lens, aperture, exposure, etc. It also goes without saying that this kind of mastery is not gained in a day. In the beginning the photographer has the same kind of problem as that involved in learning to drive a car: he is faced with a multiplicity of operations that must be co-ordinated into a smoothly functioning whole. With practice, these things become second nature. The driver ceases to think in terms of brake, clutch, and gear; his mind dictates where the car shall go and the necessary operations automatically follow. The photographer no longer has to ask himself, What lens shall I use? What exposure shall I give? Shall I use a filter? He visualizes the finished print he wants, complete to the last detail, and the operations necessary to achieve that print are carried out without need for conscious thought about them. Until a photographer has achieved this disciplined co-ordination, he cannot have full command of his medium, and his work will be governed to a greater or lesser degree by the accidental. When he has achieved it, the quantity as well as the quality of his work will be limited only by his ability to see—by the quantity and quality of his vision.

THE PICTURES: My project was officially titled THE MAKING OF A SERIES OF PHOTOGRAPHS OF THE WEST, which, translated into unofficial terms, meant traveling where I pleased and photographing whatever I wanted to photograph. I chose to concentrate on California for several reasons. First, the high cost of a photography-travel project could be somewhat reduced by working in a territory where I had bases with darkrooms available, and where the weather would permit camping out most of the year. Second, I knew enough of this state to realize it held such a rich variety of material, I could not exhaust it in ten years.

The second largest state in the Union, its 158,297 square miles contain such extremes of contrast that it is a never-failing source of delight to the statisticians of the Amazing-But-True School. In their zeal they frequently carry things too far: the juxtaposition of the United States' highest and lowest points (Mt. Whitney—14,495 feet above sea level; Badwater, in Death Valley, 279.8 feet below) has been so played upon that one expects to find the Badwater puddle at the foot of Mt. Whitney, instead of a hundred miles away across a couple of mountain ranges. Nevertheless, you cannot travel very far in California without being impressed by its startling array of contrasts; without beginning to believe that whatever exists in the rest of the world—from glacier to active volcano—is somewhere represented here.

So nature and the Boundary Commission provided me with a region of concentrated riches in which to put my photographic theory to the test. The reproductions in this book represent but a fraction of the result. Their selection was a difficult task.

As nearly as possible in that limited number, I have tried to present a cross section of the work, taking the minor notes with the major ones to round out the picture. These are not my "Hundred Best Photographs," nor do they make up a full-length picture of California, or even a full-length picture of California as I have seen it. They are a compromise of all these selecting-viewpoints, and a shorthand résumé of the two most prolific years of my photographic life.

THE TECHNICAL ASPECTS: Because I think 99/100ths of the conventional *data* given with photographic reproductions is valueless if not actually misleading, I am confining this section to a general account of my procedure and problems. All photographs reproduced in this book (and all made in the two years) were made with the following equipment:

Camera: 8x10

Lenses: a triple convertible 12″ with elements of 21″—28″

   a single element 19″

Film: Panchromatic

I carried three filters altogether, starting out with a K2 and a G, later adding an A

Films were tray-developed by inspection in Pyro Soda

Prints were made on glossy Chloride paper (ninety per cent of them on normal grade) developed in Amidol

Now to examine the results in the light of my mass-production theory—did I succeed? The answer is yes and no. From the two years' work I have destroyed few negatives because I thought my seeing was inadequate; more (but no great number) for errors due to carelessness—using the wrong scale, forgetting to stop down, double exposures (of the last, three only). The major tragedy in this class occurred in the coast redwoods where fully a third of my negatives were lost by the tripod sinking in the soft turf during the long exposures. But in spite of these mistakes, had all failures been limited to such circumstances within my control, the record would have been a shining one.

Except for occasional fast-moving subject matter—animals, clouds, waves, etc.— I made no duplicate negatives. Ninety-nine per cent of my negatives are composed to the edge of the plate—I have used that size so long, I seldom see things in another size or shape. This means that every square inch of every negative I made counted in the final result; that every mechanical error or defect meant a real loss. And—mechanically— I had very bad luck; so bad, it amounted to a two-year jinx. First it was film defects, which I did my best to trace to myself before blaming the factory which, as it happened, was the guilty party. But an admission of factory fault is small consolation for ruined, and unrepeatable negatives. My two shutters—one of them brand new, both supposed to be good ones—were continually getting out of order. Wire releases always broke at a critical moment. I had focussing difficulties which I blamed on my eyes; I got new glasses and the trouble persisted; not until the Guggenheim was over did I discover that the trouble lay in the lens—the product of a reputable firm, that had, on this of all occasions, sent out a dud.

The various trials I went through with films and papers would fill a volume, and nothing is gained by going into them here. I have said this much concerning the technical problems to show one thing: that while I still think my theory is sound, it demands for its perfect illustration in practice a better set of photographic implements than were then at my disposal. However, in fairness to manufacturers in general, I should add that working under such swiftly varying conditions of altitude, temperature, humidity, etc., was the severest kind of test for all of my equipment.

With this qualification, then, I proved the theory to my own satisfaction. Of course, if I started out now, with the added knowledge and experience acquired in those two years, I could do a better job. No honest worker can ever be completely satisfied with his results, because there is always room to go ahead.